This book is dedicated to my talented
and loving wife, Frannie.

ISBN 978-1-4507-5349-4 | Copyright © 2010
Second Printing 2011 | Printed in the United States of America | All rights reserved
Available at Amazon.com and the Kindle Store

Table of Contents

"The race is not always to the swift, but to those who keep on running"

James J. Maguire

Founder, Philadelphia Insurance Companies

Introduction

This is the story of a very ordinary couple who achieved extraordinary success in business, family, and life. When I sat down to write my story, I knew the history of the company and my family were inseparable. What happened, and how it impacted both the company and my family, for posterity, needs to be told. Along the way there were many events, heartaches, challenges, and sheer force of will that came to shape the culture and success of Philadelphia Insurance Companies and my family of high achievers.

▶ **Jim and Frannie Maguire**

Early on, running the business was simple, and the fear of the unknown was quickly replaced with the enthusiasm of new horizons. I was a natural salesman, blessed with a solid business education, grounded in Jesuit training, which was, and has forever been, my moral compass. There were non-negotiable standards of integrity, professionalism, physical fitness, and fair play, all of which remain core values in our company today.

I've often wondered about, but regularly prayed a prayer of thanksgiving for, those events and people that helped me along the way. I was fortunate to survive my own weaknesses by surrounding myself with winners, the most important of whom I readily acknowledge to be my wife, Frannie, who made me believe in myself. She was and is the focal point of my life. As my business grew, dreams of greater success were fueled by a willingness to challenge myself and move out of my comfort zone. It was dreaming that pushed me to buy my first insurance company, and dreaming that took me to Wall Street and a public offering (IPO). It's been said that there is power in positive thinking, and I am a living example of it.

You will read about the countless serendipitous events and people that blessed me, all of which I believe were "moments of grace." How else can one explain what led me to Saint Joseph's University or exposed me to the deaf community, which would forever define my business career in niche marketing. And yes, there were also those terrible dark days, losing my company and everything I owned, only to go on to greater heights. Looking back over the past 50 years has, in itself, been a defining experience.

"Discipline:
The act of accepting
responsibility"

James J. Maguire
Founder, Philadelphia Insurance Companies

Chapter 1
From Lazing to Living

▸ July 2009 - The Maguire Castle in Enniskellen, Fermanagh, Ireland
The Maguires immigrated to America in 1854 from Enniskellen.

I t's often said that families are bridges linking one's past and future. My own future began at a hospital in Philadelphia on January 7, 1934. I entered this world as the fourth child of Thomas J. and Ruth M. Maguire, younger brother of Tom, Jean, and Joan. Soon, Carol and Mike arrived, making me a big brother in a close family bound together by the strength of my parents' character.

My father was born in 1907, the first of Frank and Margaret Maguire's nine children. His parents were first-generation Irish-Americans from Enniskellen, County Fermanagh. Home for my father and his family was a rented, five-bedroom row house on Devon Street in Philadelphia's Germantown section. The house was about eight miles from the city's center. Germantown was then commonly known as Irishtown, because so many of Philadelphia's 70,000 Irish-born citizens lived there. The neighborhood erupted with family life made up of large, mostly Catholic families like the nine siblings in my father's family. In 1924, at the age of 39, my Grandfather Frank died suddenly of a heart attack. Overnight, 17-year-old Tommy, as my father was known then, became the man of the house.

Dad's income from odd jobs wasn't enough to support the family. So my Grandmother Margaret went to work as a laundress. Her sister, Kitty Walker, moved in with them to help out. The house on Devon Street was crowded. Measuring 20 feet wide and 38 feet deep, it consisted of a living room, very small dining room, and kitchen on the main floor, with three bedrooms on the second and two on the third. It had only one bathroom. Shoehorning nine Maguires and Aunt Kit into this small space left little room for privacy. Aunt Kit was a spinster and spent most of her time in the dimly lit kitchen that backed up to the laundry, where my grandmother worked in what today would be called a sweat shop, with concrete floors, mountains of laundry, no windows and certainly no air conditioning. The only "heat" in the winter came from the crowded laundry machines.

For the next five years, my father and grandmother kept the family afloat, but there was no money for anything other than the basics. The deplorable conditions at the laundry took their toll on my grandmother, who died of double pneumonia at age 46.

Although he graduated from high school, college was out of the question for my father. Though he always regretted being unable to get a better education, his outgoing personality was enough to win the affection of my mother, Ruth M. Durkin, a pretty young nurse with the faith and courage to put love before money. Her father, Daniel, was an Irish immigrant. Her mother, Alfreida, was the daughter of German immigrants who had settled in Milwaukee before Alfreida was born.

My Grandfather Durkin's first home in the United States was New York City. He was one of the many Irish laborers who helped build Saint Patrick's Cathedral. He and Alfreida were married in Milwaukee in 1906 and my mother was born a year later, on March 31, 1907. When Alfreida died in 1912, giving birth to her second child, my Aunt Helen, both girls were sent to live on a farm with Alfreida's mother, Wilomena Conrad. They stayed with her for almost three years until Ruth reached school age. Living in the country, there were few options for Ruth's education, and Wilomena didn't want to split up the sisters. So Ruth and Helen were sent to Saint Mary's, a Catholic girls' boarding school in Milwaukee, where they remained for 13 years.

In 1925, after graduating from Saint Mary's, my mother had no place to go, so when three of her girlfriends were going to study nursing at Saint Joseph's Hospital in Philadelphia, she went along. In 1927, at one of the hospital's weekend socials, she met my father. They were instantly attracted to each other. At 5 feet, 10 inches tall, Tom was handsome and fit, with a runner's body that he earned by competing as a miler for his high-school track team. Long after his track days were over, he continued to run on a regular basis. The lean but shapely Ruth stood 5 feet, 6 inches. She was a brunette with short, curly hair.

Less than two years after they met, Tom and Ruth were married in a small wedding at Saint Vincent's Catholic Church in Germantown. Ruth was attended by two of her nursing classmates, while Tom's brothers, Frank and Jim, served as the best man and groomsman. The date was May 25, 1929, five months before Black Tuesday, the day the Great Depression officially began in the United States.

The newlyweds borrowed a car from my Uncle Jim and drove to Atlantic City for a weekend honeymoon. Two days were all they could manage. Jim needed his car back, and my father and mother had to get back to work.

▶ 1925 - Ruth Durkin

Unlike many Depression-era couples, both my parents had jobs. My mother was a nurse, and my father was an insurance agent. He had been hired by Metropolitan Life (Met Life) just before their wedding. Given the times, his sales were sparse, but they got by. As the hard times got harder, though, my parents found themselves facing challenges for which they weren't prepared and couldn't have imagined.

▶ 1929 - Ruth (center) with bridesmaids

Born of the Depression

I was born in 1934, the height of the Depression. My parents already had three children, a boy, Tom, aged two, and 13-month-old twin girls, Jean and Joan. Money was scarce and my mother, frugal by nature, refused to turn the heat above 62 degrees. She also kept most of the lights off in our small, rented row house in Upper Darby, Pennsylvania.

The house had several more square feet of floor space than the one in which my father had grown up, but with four children, it still felt cramped. The house had four bedrooms located above the living room, kitchen, and dining room. A shed-like structure off the kitchen served as a pantry and housed the icebox. The iceman climbed the 20 steps from the back alley to make his deliveries every morning. Beneath the pantry and kitchen was a one-car garage, where my father kept his 1938 black Chrysler sedan.

When we children had nothing else to do, we made our own fun. On Saturdays, we walked the short distance from our house to 69th Street, which was full of shops and movie theaters. We would linger near the back of a theater until the door swung open. As moviegoers came out, we slipped in. The sports biography of *Knute Rockne: All American* was a movie I went back to see three times; *The Grapes of Wrath* was another favorite. On hot summer days, we ran behind the iceman's wagon picking up stray ice chips.

My father didn't have the luxury of pursuing carefree pastimes. He spent most of his time going from door to door to collect 50-cent premiums. In the height of the Depression in 1934, customers were cashing in their policies, thus putting Met Life under enormous cash pressure which almost caused him to lose his job.

My brother and I always had a paper route or some other paying job, like shagging golf balls at the country-club driving range. Picking up balls and putting them in a bag that had to be dragged back to the pro shop was tough work, and it didn't pay much. Only boys who were too small to caddy shagged balls. When I was big enough to carry a bag of clubs for 18 holes, I thought I had struck it rich.

I turned over every cent I earned to my mother. She kept amazingly detailed financial records, which featured individual accounts for each of us. I learned quickly to be thrifty and remain so to this day. If I wanted a new baseball glove or sneakers, my mother took me shopping and deducted the amount I spent from my account.

In eighth grade, I wanted a new bike, so I set out to find one I liked and could afford. That summer, I finally bought a blue Schwinn classic cruiser, equipped with a mirror, headlight, and rack over the rear tire – but only after Ruth lent me $15, which I quickly paid back from my paper-route income.

Northward and Upward Bound

In December 1941, the Japanese attacked Pearl Harbor and the draft was enacted. My father was well within the age for conscription but fortunately for us – in fact, because of us – he was granted a deferment. The military didn't draft men with large families. Also, he was partially deaf.

My father was promoted that year to field training instructor at Met Life and was transferred to Albany, New York. For the next seven years, he traveled the Eastern seaboard. We lived about 10 miles outside Albany, in Averill Park, a small, mostly dairy-farming community of about 300. With the farms so spread out, we had few friends.

We lived in a rented, semi-detached house next door to Saint Henry's Catholic Church, where we attended Mass every Sunday morning and where I learned to be an altar server. Although I wasn't a good student and struggled with reading and spelling, I managed to memorize the Latin responses of the liturgy, which pleased Mom and Dad.

Our house included a stand-alone four-car garage and a barn, its second-floor hayloft a source of endless hours of entertainment. A chicken coop attached to the barn housed about 30 hens that provided us with fresh eggs. When the hens stopped laying, they became fried chicken. We had five acres of tillable land on which we planted corn, tomatoes, carrots, and squash. Even though my father's promotion came with a raise, we still enjoyed growing our own food. Learning all the lessons that nature teaches those who plant and harvest and care for animals was invaluable for us. As a father later in life, I would purchase a farm and pass on to my children some of the very same lessons.

We worked hard, and when the work was done, we played hard, too. Nearby Crystal Lake had a beach where visitors could rent sailboats and paddle boats and a bathhouse for changing and showering at day's end. It also had a merry-go-round and concessions that sold ice cream, cotton candy, and hot dogs.

My father was a fitness buff, always working hard to stay in shape. He regularly swam across Crystal Lake and back on summer Saturday afternoons. My brother Tom rowed a boat beside him. As much as we enjoyed the activities at Crystal Lake, we also saw it as an opportunity to make some money. I collected tickets on the merry-go-round, my sisters worked in the bathhouse and concession stand, and my brother rented out boats.

When summer was over, we all went back to school. The four oldest children – Tom, Jean, Joan, and I – spent our first year in Averill Park at the local public school. We then transferred to Saint Mary's Catholic School in Troy, New York, where I was required to repeat the third grade.

Most of our extended family still lived in Philadelphia, and the majority of our school friends were nine miles away in Troy. So my brothers and sisters and I mostly kept to ourselves. Being

▸ **Crystal Lake Amusement Park**
We also saw it as an opportunity to make some money.
I collected tickets on the merry-go-round.

▸ **1949 - Rochester, NY, Easter**
Jimmy and Mother

alone most of the time made me independent. I did befriend a local boy, Ronnie Rescott, with whom I fished, hunted, and trapped muskrats. Though muskrat trapping was strictly a winter activity, it was a lucrative one. I earned $3 for each pelt. One of us would walk the lake every morning to check our traps. One winter we sold 30 pelts.

School was difficult for me but no one at home seemed particularly concerned, even though I repeated third grade. My bad report cards didn't prompt much of a response. "Study harder and longer," I was told, but then I was left to my own devices. None of my teachers took much of an interest, either. At the time, lower-grade classes in parochial schools typically numbered 50 to 60 students supervised by one harried nun. Slow learners were assumed to be lazy, stupid, or both, and simply passed over. Because my brothers and sisters did well in school, it was assumed that I was just the dumb one in the house.

Years later, I was diagnosed with a reading disorder broadly referred to as dyslexia. But in the early 1940s, teachers didn't know that children who couldn't read or spell were neurologically handicapped. At home, my mother seldom had me read aloud because she knew I had difficulty reading and didn't want to embarrass me in front of my siblings. (Therapists have since learned that reading aloud is actually a favored exercise for treating and teaching reading skills.)

In 1947, my father was promoted again, this time to the position of manager of the Rochester, New York, office of Met Life. That meant another move for our family and another new school for me.

When we left Averill Park, part of our family would remain behind in the graveyard of Saint Henry's. Ruth's final pregnancy – her ninth in 13 years – ended in tragedy. The baby died in the first week after birth. The quiet funeral and burial were marked by tremendous sadness.

Years later, I was diagnosed with a reading disorder broadly referred to as dyslexia.

I spent the final year of middle school at Sacred Heart Parochial on Flower City Parkway, which was run by the Sisters of Saint Joseph. "Order is Heaven's first law" was engraved atop the front door, and they took this very seriously. If you were deemed to be out of order for any reason or broke a rule, punishment was swift and sometimes severe. You might be sent for a lengthy stay in a darkened coat closet or kept after school to clean the blackboards or sweep the floor. Roughhousing during recess could get you three sharp smacks with a yardstick on the palm of your hand.

I will always remember the day I talked back to Sister Rose Marie. Without warning in front of my 8th-grade class, she hauled off and cracked me across the face. I probably deserved it, but the shock gave me a lasting respect for authority.

Achievement and Heartbreak

In 1949, as a reward for 20 years of travel and loyal service, my father was named a regional manager for upstate New York, and we had to move yet again, this time to Utica, New York. The promotion was a big deal for Dad. Two years later, his "outstanding success" was recognized at a banquet Met Life held in his honor.

We were very proud of my father's success, but academically, I paid a dear price for it. I had drifted through six schools in 10 years, never

▸ **1950 - My Dad being honored by Met Life**

learning to read or spell. None of the schools seemed more than a rest stop on the way to another city. Then came Utica. It was the cradle of a new life for me. My four years at Saint Francis de Sales High School – plus the constant encouragement and example of my father who always took time weekly to exercise – switched me from lazing to living, from wasting to winning.

I quickly gained acceptance at Saint Francis de Sales. Boys and girls were segregated and the Franciscan Brothers taught the boys. My academics improved in the following years because the class sizes were smaller and I received one-on-one tutoring.

I worked hard making friends and played hard on the gridiron, the hardwood, and the diamond. With the same fiercely competitive attitude as my father, I wanted to win at everything.

In the spring of 1952, my senior year, I co-captained the Saint Francis basketball team, and we won the city championship. My father, dressed in coat and tie, came to all of my games and cheered me on. Afterwards, he and I had long discussions, dissecting various plays and talking about what I could have done better.

T. J. Maguire, Life Insurance Manager, 45

T. J. Maguire

Thomas J. Maguire, 45, of 67 Oxford Rd., New Hartford, died June 24, 1952, in St. Elizabeth Hospital. The Utica district manager for Metropolitan Life Insurance Co., he had been ill seven days.

▸ Died June 24th, 1952

He had always been my anchor, but he grew more important to me during those moments of shared experience and insight. "You've got to believe in yourself," he invariably said after reviewing a game.

Brucker, Lemke, Maguire, Nicknish and O'Halloran. Coach Fran Klein outlining a bit of strategy to his starting five just before the opening whistle of the City Championship game.

Saint Francis was indispensable to my growth. But the main reason I came into my own was my father. At 45 and on his way to possibly running Met Life, he was proof that persistence, integrity, and loyalty to a cause lead to success. As my self-confidence grew, my academic performance improved, too. How great life was – until it wasn't. "Life changes in an instant," Joan Didion once wrote, "an ordinary instant." And so it was for me.

In mid-June, the week before graduation, my father fell ill with a fever and was hospitalized. The doctors initially suspected sunstroke – he had spent the day before in his garden where he acquired a nasty sunburn. Later, they realized he had spinal meningitis. None of us, least of all me, occupied as I was with graduation activities, realized the seriousness of the situation.

My father was under sedation but supposedly all right when I stopped in to see him the morning of June 24, 1952. When I entered his room, he was half asleep. "Jimmy's here," my mother told him (those words echoed in my head for years), and he nodded his head as if he understood her. Not wanting to disturb him, I only stayed for a few minutes. Mom told me she would be staying with him. My sisters Jean and Joan would attend my graduation in her stead.

Even by the standards of those days, my father's passing was premature at age 45. Grief and shock engulfed us.

On graduation night, I stayed out for hours, giving no thought to what might be happening at the hospital or at home. At 2 A.M., when I finally reached our front door, my mother and brothers and sisters came to meet me. Their faces ashen, they broke the almost incomprehensible news that my father had died. My mother was inconsolable, and my brothers and sisters were confused and scared.

"You'll Never Walk Alone"

Even by the standards of those days, my father's passing was premature at age 45. Grief and shock engulfed us. Standing-room-only crowds descended on the wake and funeral at Saint John the Evangelist Church in Utica. At the wake, Cecil J. North, the executive vice president of Metropolitan Life who would later become its president, praised my father, saying that he was destined for a leadership role at the company. His tribute was a source of pride and comfort to us all.

My mother asked me to go with my Uncle Jack on the train that carried the body back to Philadelphia. My brother Tom drove the rest of the family to Philadelphia. I watched as the casket was loaded on the baggage car for the long, slow ride to New York City. There, we transferred to a Philadelphia-bound train. When we arrived, my mother and the entire family were waiting to meet us. But the casket wasn't on the train. Without telling us, the railroad had transferred it from our passenger train to one that carried freight. It would not arrive until the following morning. Certain that I was somehow responsible, I agonized over the mistake.

I should have been on guard, I thought, to protect my father as he protected me.

The two-day wake and funeral were enormous. At Nichols Funeral Home, the line on the first night took up an entire city block. Approximately 500 people showed up. Father Frank Atmore, my father's cousin, officiated at the funeral Mass in Germantown's Saint Vincent's Church, the same church where Mom and Dad were married. Finally, my father was buried alongside other family members at Holy Sepulchre Cemetery in Philadelphia.

For a full month after my father's death, we were inundated with an outpouring of visitors, cards, letters, and other expressions of sympathy. Scores of messages came from business associates, praising him for his goodness and honesty. But my mother never actually spoke to us children about the tragedy we were enduring. In those days, mourning was private, feelings were suppressed, and thoughts were left unspoken.

I knew I was expected to act like a man, helping to take responsibility for the family, but I was gripped by a combination of sadness, fear, and loss of direction. It was my father who had given me confidence and taught me to believe in myself. He was my compass. All I could think of then, and for a long time after, were the lyrics of "You'll Never Walk Alone," the song my class had chosen as our graduation theme. I knew that Dad would want me to hold "my head up high," just as the song says, walking "on through the wind [and] the rain . . . with hope in [my] heart." I wanted to believe that his words and his memory would see me through whatever came my way, and that I would never walk alone. But my self-confidence was newfound and easily shaken. Not a good sign for a young man about to enter college.

Niagara, Here I Come (and Go)

My father's two sisters and five brothers all urged my mother to return to Philadelphia. She agreed. So the house in Utica was sold, and we moved back to Pennsylvania. My mother purchased a four-bedroom home in Havertown, a Philadelphia suburb, and we settled in. The house was modest, but the backyard opened onto a 40-acre park that was seldom used, making it a good place for my younger sister, Carol, and brother Mike to play. My brother Tom returned to Rochester, where his high school friends and future wife, Mary Ellen Creedon, lived.

Mother was 45 years old, jobless, and responsible for the care and feeding of five children. But she also prided herself on coping with whatever obstacles God put in her path. At the time, I was too young and immature to see how frightened she must have been under the iron veneer she presented.

In early August of 1952, John J. "Taps" Gallagher, Niagara University's basketball coach, called me. He had seen the Saint Francis de Sales championship game and was offering me an athletic scholarship to Niagara. It was an all-male Catholic school situated four miles north of Niagara Falls. But with no money for room and board, I couldn't go unless I found additional help.

My mother contacted my father's cousin, Father Frank Atmore, the priest who conducted the funeral Mass, and, as luck would have it, dean of students at Niagara. Father Atmore was willing to help and got me a work-study scholarship to cover the rest of my expenses. I was assigned the 6:30 A.M. breakfast shift in the dining room two mornings a week, keeping the buffet tables stocked, wiping down trays, clearing tables, and emptying trash cans. At Sunday night dinner, I would be a gofer, scrubbing up after people.

I arrived at Niagara on August 15, 1952, excited to play basketball. Within days of starting practice, I jumped from the freshman squad to the varsity team. I played with them until the Christmas break. Despite my athletic success, I missed my family and continued to grieve for my father. Without him, I lost direction. I still wanted to play well, but I was academically over my head. My grades reflected my bleak mood. I had taken only four courses that first semester, and, at the end of it, I had a dismal grade point average of 1.7

My report card arrived during the Christmas break. It was accompanied by a letter saying that I was on academic probation and ineligible to play basketball. My mother was unhappy with my grades, and I was unhappy that Niagara wouldn't let me play ball. Mom and I concluded that curing my homesickness might get me back on track, so we decided to visit Saint Joseph's University, then an all-male Jesuit commuter school in Philadelphia.

Father Matt Sullivan, the dean of students, was welcoming and sympathetic to the loss of my father the day we visited in early January. But he was skeptical of my chances at Saint Joe's. So my mother made my case: "It's important for him to stay home," she said. "His grades at Niagara were largely a result of his father's death. His family would be a stabilizing influence on him." Father Sullivan was sold, and I was accepted on a trial basis.

I started as a full-time student during the spring semester of 1953. But the problems that had plagued me at Niagara quickly returned. I was having a hard time academically and having trouble making friends. My classmates who came from the local high schools had begun their first year together the previous semester. They all knew each other and I was an outsider. From the outset I felt marginalized – also, I was still ineligible to play basketball until the fall semester.

▶ 1953 - Summer

All in all, my first semester performance at Saint Joseph's was as unimpressive as my Niagara showing had been. Elated to receive the first B of my college career, in American history, I was, in turn, deflated by the D's I earned in religion, geometry, and science. I totally failed British poetry, a subject that required reading aloud in class – something I could not do then and probably still couldn't do today.

The summer after transferring to Saint Joe's, I pumped gas during the week and went to the Jersey Shore on the weekends. Four of my buddies and I rented a small apartment in the seaside resort of Ocean City. It was a famously dry town, but that didn't stop us from having our fun. One of the guys had a car, and we drove to Somers Point, our favorite nightspot, where several bars attracted a college crowd. Drinking beer and carousing late into the night was our standard behavior.

Booting me out of the house and the university turned out to be the best things anyone ever did for me.

One Saturday night, my friend Nick Breslin and I got into a scuffle with a couple of guys. All four of us wound up in jail and stayed there until my mother drove from Philadelphia on Sunday afternoon to bail me out. When she arrived, she paid the $350 bond and completed the paperwork, establishing my hearing date on charges of disorderly conduct. Later that summer, I returned to Somers Point for my court appearance before a local judge. In addition to the $350 fine, I was banned from town for the balance of the season. My mother and I hardly spoke for the rest of the summer, and every cent I made pumping gas went to her until the $350 was completely paid. It wasn't the money that hurt, though, it was me inflicting pain on my mother, who was living with the pain of my father's death. What a jerk I was!

At War with Myself

Near the end of June 1950, hostilities broke out in Korea. My draft notice arrived in late April of 1954, and I went to the dean's office to apply for a student deferment. Father Sullivan wanted to talk to my mother before signing it. What Mom didn't know was that when mid-term marks arrived in December, I had intercepted the envelope. I had four D's in my business courses and an F in French – well under the 2.0 average I needed to automatically secure a deferment. I panicked. With a careful hand, I changed all five grades to B's, resealed the envelope, and left it on the table with the other mail. When my mother opened it, she was overjoyed. She told me I was finally getting my act together. In our meeting about the deferment, Father Sullivan explained to Ruth that my GPA was 1.6. She went pale and said nothing.

Having lost all credibility with Father Sullivan, and knowing that Mom was stunned, I was frozen out of the conversation about my future. Sullivan asked her if she would support his decision not to sign my deferment, a move he said that would certainly lead to my being drafted. Mom readily agreed, and for good reason. She was fed up with me and upset that I had deceived her. I was wasting my time and tuition money, but more importantly, I'd lost all credibility with her. She didn't want me living at home anymore. The ride home from Saint Joe's that day was the longest 20 minutes of my life.

Booting me out of the house and the university turned out to be the best things anyone ever did for me. Seeing how I hurt my Mother was a lasting lesson of the importance of integrity. The regimentation, discipline, and physical challenges of the military were just what I needed.

▶ **Fr. Matthew Sullivan, S.J., Dean of Students**
Booting me out of Saint Joseph's led to my conscription in the Army – an experience that changed my life.

"You must believe to achieve"

James J. Maguire
Founder, Philadelphia Insurance Companies

Chapter 2
The College Try (Again)

▶ Japanese Naval Academy, Hiroshima
I attended clerk typist school, September 1954. The dining rooms were appointed with crisp, white tablecloths, and our meals were served by Japanese waiters wearing white gloves and high-collared black coats.

June 24, 1954, was the second anniversary of my father's death. It was also the day I was conscripted into the U.S. Army. I reported to Fort Dix in New Jersey. There, I was taught how to shoot and salute, though not in that order.

During basic training, I played for the Fort Dix 8th Army football team and signed up for jump school. I hoped to join the 82nd Airborne Division, but before I ever got the chance to pull a ripcord, I fractured my right heel and landed in the hospital. I had been learning how to hit the ground and roll by jumping off successively higher platforms into a pit of sawdust. I had flown through the air for all of 15 feet. In the end, the fracture turned out to be a lucky break.

Unable to ship out with my unit, I was dispatched to Tacoma, Washington, after my cast came off. Less than a month later, I boarded a troopship with 6,000 other soldiers headed for Korea. It was a cold and miserable trip lasting a little less than two weeks. The food was okay but starchy, and some men were seasick all day, every day. We slept below deck in hammocks strung four deep and endured long lines for the showers and toilets, located another level down. Any modesty you had was quickly flushed away.

Soon after boarding ship, I attended Sunday Mass. I noticed that the chaplain didn't have an altar server, so I volunteered. For the rest of the trip, I served the daily and Sunday Masses. In gratitude, the priest, Father Kevin Laughry, let me use his private shower and bathroom and invited me to eat with him in his cabin several times a week.

All along, I assumed I would be stationed in Korea. But, in December, when the ship anchored in Tokyo Bay to take on supplies, several of us who had played college sports were bused to Hiroshima and housed at the Japanese Naval Academy, then occupied by the U.S. Army. The brass had picked us to play sports for the 8th Army's teams.

The Naval Academy, located on Hiroshima Bay, was as immaculate as it was beautiful, with stately marble buildings and manicured grounds. The dining rooms were appointed with crisp, white tablecloths, and our meals were served by waiters wearing black coats and white gloves. Our rooms, bathrooms, and showers were cleaned by Japanese house boys every day. It wasn't your typical Army life, for sure. I attended typist school for eight weeks as part of my training before being transferred to Camp Zama outside of Yokohama, the headquarters of the 8th Army.

At Camp Zama, I was assigned to a desk job in the office of military history. We practiced sports every day, which meant my office duties ended at noon; but because I was a privileged athlete, I also was responsible for leading calisthenics at 6 A.M. each morning, before breakfast, from a 15-foot platform. I loved the 25 minutes of responsibility and exercise. I found myself playing in some of the toughest games of my life. One of our football teammates, Art Hunter, went on to suit up as a tackle for the Cleveland Browns. Another, Mike Tackus, played guard for the New York Giants. On our basketball team, we were lucky to have a point guard who had been coached by the legendary Adolph Rupp at the University of Kentucky.

During the fall 1955 season, we won the football championship and were named the best team in the Far East Command. I was elated. More important, as with my high school athletic experiences, I was starting to regain my self-confidence.

Not all my memories of the two years in Japan involved sports. On a regular basis, I participated in military maneuvers, which included overnight bivouac, hiking, and rifle range qualifying. My least favored job was guard duty, which included walking the perimeter of the camp and on several occasions guarding prisoners on a work detail. Military prison personnel were routinely sent out during the day to clean up, pick up, paint, or dig. Whatever the job, six prisoners were assigned to one guard for the day. You were told if anybody escaped, you'd serve their time. True or not (I never found out), it sure did get your attention.

▶ Mt. Fuji
In late fall 1955, a group of us tried to climb Mt. Fuji.

I left the base whenever I could. One exceptional adventure was an attempt to scale Mount Fuji. It was late fall, and a group of us decided to make the climb. I've never forgotten the mountain's starkness and severity. Before we reached the summit, a heavy storm blew in, and we were forced to spend the night in a rickety emergency shelter. There were probably 60 or so climbers who took refuge that night. Picture a one-room, 40-foot by 40-foot, single-story wood building with two lights at either end of the room. A pile of blankets to spread on the floor, for sleeping, were in a bin. When we lay down to sleep, we were a sea of bodies with little room to even roll over. We had candy bars and rain apparel in our backpacks which gave us some comfort and nourishment before trying in vain to get some sleep. The following morning we returned to Zama tired and feeling defeated.

The routine at Camp Zama was physically demanding, but I enjoyed it. Since the camp was only 18 miles from Tokyo, we often went into the city on weekends we didn't have military duty or a game. A strong U.S. dollar made it possible for us to stay Friday and Saturday nights at the elegant, and now sadly demolished, Frank Lloyd Wright-designed Imperial Hotel. Like young soldiers everywhere, we drank too much and generally raised hell. (A lingering sign of my immaturity.)

Chances and Choices

Before marching me off to boot camp in the summer of 1954, Father Sullivan had thrown me a lifeline, and I clung to it during my two years in the service. He had said that after my Army tour was up, I could enroll for the summer semester at Saint Joseph's. I would be on academic probation, but he said if I passed my summer courses, I could continue as a junior. He also recommended that I take a correspondence course in reading, knowing my skills would have to improve if I were ever going to finish college. Father Sullivan had been advised that I did not have college-level reading ability. So during my tour of duty I enrolled in a University of California correspondence course entitled, "First Year Reading and Composition." I passed with a C.

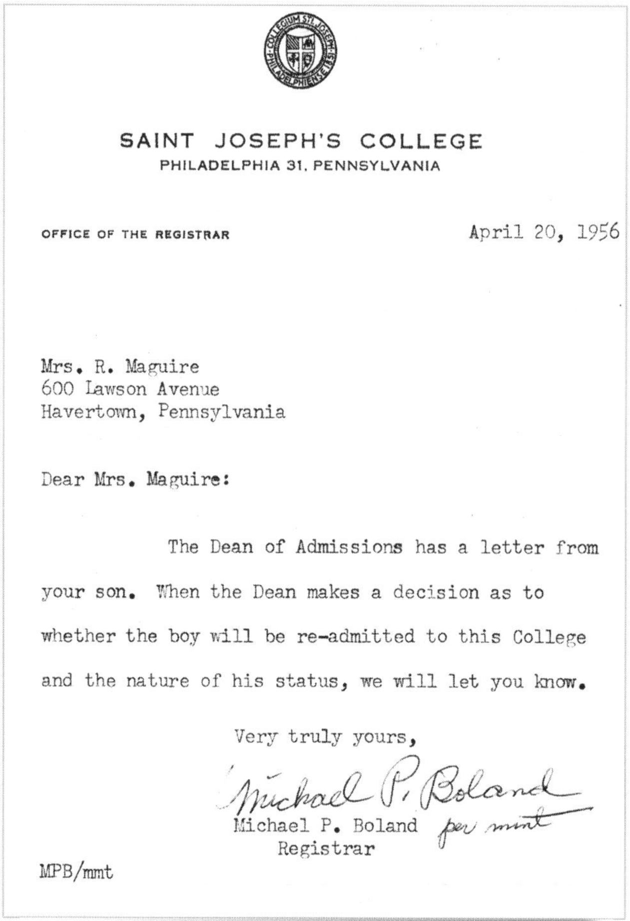

SAINT JOSEPH'S COLLEGE
PHILADELPHIA 31, PENNSYLVANIA

OFFICE OF THE REGISTRAR   April 20, 1956

Mrs. R. Maguire
600 Lawson Avenue
Havertown, Pennsylvania

Dear Mrs. Maguire:

The Dean of Admissions has a letter from your son. When the Dean makes a decision as to whether the boy will be re-admitted to this College and the nature of his status, we will let you know.

Very truly yours,

Michael P. Boland per mmt
Michael P. Boland
Registrar

MPB/mmt

▶ "The Boy"
I was stunned! I was no longer a BOY and I did have a promise.

But, as the spring of 1956 approached, I was offered another sort of lifeline. I had three days off and decided to go to Nagasaki, but I took six and ended up AWOL. For God knows what reason, the captain of my division put me on house arrest for seven days and handed me re-enlistment papers. He made it clear that if I signed up for four more years, I'd be sent to officer training school. I liked the idea of being an Army officer. I could almost picture my mother standing at our front door, smiling proudly and welcoming home the be-medaled first lieutenant I had become. But this was a time for rational thinking, not daydreaming.

I consider myself lucky, but I also know that sometimes you have to make your own luck.

Shortly before being offered the chance to become an officer, and about two months before I was due to be discharged, I wrote to Father Sullivan to confirm that I would be admitted to the June 1956 summer session as promised. Mike Boland, the registrar, wrote back to my mother saying, "When the dean makes a decision as to whether the boy will be readmitted and the nature of his status, we will let you know." I was stunned, but I refused to accept his apparent change of heart. In my reply I wrote, "I do not feel that my two years of college were a total loss, and you did promise me a chance at summer school."

If he rejected my request, there was no way my unit would discharge me early – in time to begin summer school. In that event, I thought officer training school might be a good choice after all. Still, I knew in my heart that I didn't want a career in the military.

I consider myself lucky, but I also know that sometimes you have to make your own luck. And that's what I did when I poured my heart out to the Jesuit chaplain at Camp Zama and asked him to write a letter to Father Sullivan on my behalf. Whether the outcome was all about one Jesuit doing a favor for another, I'll never know. But my choice of an advocate didn't hurt my cause. Father Sullivan sent me an acceptance letter and agreed that I could return to Saint Joe's on probation for the summer session.

The Third Time a Charm

On June 24, 1956, the fourth anniversary of my father's death, I arrived home in Philadelphia and returned to college for the third time.

I completed one accounting course at Saint Joseph's, attending class four nights a week, and earned the remaining credits I needed to start the fall semester as a junior by taking two daytime classes at Temple University. I got two B's and one C that summer. And by convincing Father Sullivan to accept the University of California correspondence course, I added three more credits to my transcript.

My Army experience had driven home the point that there are no shortcuts in life...

Despite my hard work and frantic schedule, I still had a lot of catching up to do. Many of my Philadelphia friends had graduated from college, gotten jobs, or were in graduate school. Was I jealous? Yes. I was living modestly, supporting myself on the $165 a month I received under the G.I. Bill. I wanted what my friends had.

My mother was glad I was home. She was still tough as nails, but she could see I had grown up – partly as a result of a letter I had written her before I left Japan. In it, I promised to earn my college degree and do so with a 3.0 GPA. I also said that if I lived at home, I would pay rent – no more freeloading.

And to put our relationship on a new footing, one based on mutual respect, I began calling her Ruth instead of Mother after I got home. My brothers and sisters still called her Mom or Mother, but she was Ruth to me from then on. It just seemed right. It was my way of saying I'm an adult now, and she liked it.

Soon after returning to school, I found that talking about what I was reading helped my understanding and retention. So I started a study group with several other students in my accounting class. We met one weekday night and every Sunday at my house to prepare for the next week's classes. The new regimen paid off: I got a B in the course.

By the end of the fall 1956 semester, I could boast B's in accounting; business statistics; and industrial management, cost and budget control. Had it not been for my D in theology, I would have made the Dean's List.

I registered for another required theology course in the spring semester. Determined to avoid my previous problems, I spent extra time reading each and every one of the required assignments.

The result was a midterm D. I went to see my professor, Father Hunter Guthrie, chair of the university's philosophy department. I knew I could do the coursework if I devoted more time to it, and I asked Father Guthrie for help.

Father Guthrie had come to Philadelphia after serving as the president of Georgetown University. He was a big man, at least six feet, two inches tall and weighing around 240 pounds. A high forehead made him appear scholarly, but he was not the ivory-tower sort. Warm and inviting, he was intent on bringing out the best in his students. When I asked him for his assistance, he offered to tutor me outside of class.

Father Guthrie quickly saw that I needed extra time to read and comprehend at the college level. He saw that I was finger reading, pointing to one word at a time as I tried to understand the meaning of a sentence. If I didn't have my finger on each word, the lines ran together and the meaning became garbled. Always behind in my reading assignments, I often tried to skim the material which compromised my understanding.

▸ Rev. Hunter Guthrie, S.J., Chairman of Philosophy
Department - 1958

He was an early pioneer in the study of Dyslexia and the
most important and influential educator in my college career.
Under his steady hand my reading ability improved.

Father Guthrie recognized that I was unable to comprehend while reading aloud. He recommended, instead, that I use a ruler or an index card to block out the lines below the one I was reading. He also taught me how best to take notes. "Forget about speed," he often told me. "Just take your time."

Each week, he gave me reading assignments that I summarized in writing. We would meet in his tiny office to review the assignments and then do reading exercises. Initially I felt embarrassed to read aloud, but Father Guthrie quickly put me at ease.

> *"Forget about speed," he often told me.*
> *"Just take your time."*

Father Guthrie was an early pioneer in the study of teaching people who learn differently and or dyslexia. And no doubt, some of the advice and instruction he gave me may not be suitable or adequate for others. But under his steady hand my reading gradually improved and I learned how to manage my dyslexia! He truly changed my study and comprehension abilities –and yes, he gave me a B in my final theology seminar.

I already owed an enormous debt of gratitude to Father Sullivan. Now, I owed an equal one to Father Guthrie.

Frannie

Soon after I returned from Japan, I reconnected with old friends, one being Frances Mary McLaughlin. Frannie, as everyone called her, had grown up in Philadelphia and had been

▸ **Our transportation to the Shore**
Frannie next to the first car I purchased:
a 1957 black, four-door Chevy.

secretly engaged to Frank "Sugar" Lane. He gave her a ring before being drafted into the Army. But in the winter of 1955, while serving with the military police, Sugar died in an automobile accident outside Fort Hood, Texas. I had known and liked him, too. In fact, it was through Sugar that I first met Frannie.

Our relationship began slowly. Frannie had a group of friends she spent time with, and I, along with a few other Saint Joe students, began to join them for movies, ice skating, weekend parties, and trips to the Jersey Shore.

I frequently volunteered to drive her back and forth to the Shore for our group weekends. Within six months we both knew we were falling in love.

At the beginning, Ruth didn't take to Frannie (although my brothers and sisters adored her). "Too skinny to have babies," Ruth complained, adding that she was just dating me on the rebound. Also, the first time Frannie had dinner at our house, her peas went skittering across the table when her knife slipped while she was cutting her meat. (A minor infraction, to be sure, but enough to leave a poor impression with Ruth.)

My mother's reaction to Frannie, I'm sure, was more about the fact that she didn't like the loss of my attention. Ruth was alone more now that my brothers and sisters were busy with their own lives and families. Tom and his wife, Mary Ellen, had a house just outside Philadelphia and were occupied with two young children. My twin sisters, Jean and Joan, had gotten married in a double wedding in September 1956 and were starting their own households. My sister Carol, a member of the Sisters of Notre Dame, was living in Washington, D.C. Michael, my younger brother, was attending Notre Dame University in South Bend, Indiana.

What my mother couldn't see was that Frannie was the best thing that had ever happened to me. We wanted to spend all our time together, which made it difficult for me to keep up with my classes. But I managed. I balanced my work and study schedules largely because Frannie believed I could.

▶ July 1957 - Engagement party
Ruth, Jim, Frannie, and Margaret McLaughlin

Frannie and I had a lot in common. Our friends pronounced us, in the vernacular of the day, "a striking couple." She was (and is) a knockout – blonde, beautiful, and brainy. We both liked to dance and play sports, and we were both middle children in large Irish-Catholic families. Frannie had three sisters and three brothers. And, like me, she lost her father when she was 18.

But while my parents had struggled to make ends meet, Frannie's family was well-off. Her father, Edward Francis McLaughlin, was a prominent surgeon in Philadelphia before his death in 1954. He succumbed to leukemia at age 49. Her mother, Margaret Long McLaughlin, was a nurse. Frannie attended private schools – first, Mater Misericordiae Academy, then Gwynedd-Mercy College. Her family belonged to various country clubs and owned a summer home in Longport, New Jersey. Paintings by Frannie's paternal grandmother lined the walls of their home, and Frannie had been encouraged to enroll in art classes when she was young. Her parents had exposed her to the cultural events of the day.

In June of 1957, Frannie left for California to visit her sister Louise. She stayed for two weeks, and I hated being without her. Letters flew back and forth. I couldn't help sharing the good news about my spring 1957 grades:

> *"I received my Dean's List notification – the first in my life – in the mail from Saint Joe's and carried on high for two days, until people got tired of hearing about my good fortune."*

I don't remember if I ever showed Frannie my Dean's List letter, but I do recall buying a half-carat diamond ring for $300. I was so short of cash that, much to my relief, the jeweler, a friend of Frannie's family, agreed not to accept payment until she accepted my proposal.

It was midnight when I picked her up at the airport. On the drive home, I couldn't wait any longer. I pulled over on the shoulder of Philadelphia's West River Drive. "Will you marry me?" I asked. She said "yes" without hesitation. Neither of us had the slightest doubt that we were destined to be together, and the sooner we got married, the better.

Our friends seemed to agree that we were right for each other, including Dr. Jim Harris, the surgeon at Germantown Hospital who employed Frannie as his medical secretary. Dr. Harris adored her. He had been a friend of her father and trained under him. When he told Frannie that I was "just right for her," it was as if I had received her father's blessing.

Being engaged to Frannie gave me a kind of stability that I had lost after my father's death. Now I found myself enjoying pleasant evenings with her family, playing canasta with her sister Marge and Marge's fiancé, Eddie Smith.

That summer marked the beginning of what would become a deep and lasting friendship with J. Eustace Wolfington.

That summer marked the beginning of what would become a deep and lasting friendship with J. Eustace Wolfington. He was a close friend of Marge and Eddie and a fellow student at Saint Joe's. Eustace's family had been selling cars in Philadelphia for generations, and Frannie's father had been a regular customer. In addition, Frannie and Eustace's sister, Peggy Ann, were high school classmates and close friends.

To earn extra money for college, Eustace established a business selling vertical blinds. He ran it out of his father's garage, and he hired me as an installer.

I put in two days a week that summer installing blinds for Eustace. I was also back in summer school – this time at Villanova – to retake a three-credit American Literature course I had failed my sophomore year. (This time, I received a B.) And every morning starting at 4 A.M., I once again returned to a paper route: tossing copies of *The Philadelphia Inquirer* from the 1957 black, four-door Chevy I bought with my mustering-out pay from the Army. That car was the first big-ticket item I purchased after returning from Japan, and I loved it. When I wasn't working or studying, I wanted to be with Frannie.

As our wedding approached, Frannie asked her sisters to serve as maid of honor and bridesmaids. I chose as my groomsmen two of her brothers, my younger brother, Michael, and Nick Breslin, the friend who spent a night in jail with me at the Jersey Shore. I asked my brother Tom to be my best man.

▸ **Wedding - November 28, 1957**
Our first dance

Tom and I had had a somewhat strained relationship growing up. As the second son, I resented being pushed around by him. I also begrudged the fact that life for him seemed so easy. He did well in school while I struggled. Our relationship started to turn around when I returned from the military. My success at Saint Joe's and my contentment with Frannie added a layer of maturity to our relationship.

Frannie McLaughlin's Husband

On Thanksgiving Day, 1957, Frannie and I were married in a formal ceremony at Saint Madeleine Sophie Catholic Church in Philadelphia. The wedding reception was held at the Germantown Cricket Club. It was a lovely and extravagant affair, thanks in large measure to the attention and affection that Frannie's mother lavished on every detail. The event merited a half-column in the society pages of the *Germantown Courier*. It included a beautiful photograph of Frannie and a description of the bride's "long-sleeved gown of white peau de soie with appliqués of Chantilly lace around the neckline." It was actually the same dress Frannie's sister had worn at her wedding a month before ours.

For our honeymoon, we drove to Split Rock Lodge in Pennsylvania's Pocono Mountains. We stayed only three days. On Monday morning, I returned to school and Frannie was back at her desk in Dr. Harris's office.

▶ **November 1957**
Jim and Frannie's honeymoon weekend at Split Rock Lodge in the Poconos.

Before the wedding, Frannie had faithfully put away $1,500 of her salary in an account at the Germantown Savings Bank. The honeymoon cost us $150 and Frannie's engagement ring was $300 (technically, she bought her own ring), which left us with exactly $1,050. For $55 a month, we rented a three-room, third-floor walk-up apartment on the corner of Green Street and Washington Lane in Germantown. It wasn't far from the row house my parents lived in when they were first married. We furnished it with a bed, television set, kitchen table, and two chairs. It was sparse, but it was ours.

Just one thing bothered me. My wife was so well-connected and popular that I quickly became known as "Frannie McLaughlin's husband." I was irritated at first, but then it motivated me: I wanted to become successful so people would know who the hell I was.

Starting a Life and a Career

Each evening as I returned from school and climbed the stairs, I greeted the couple who lived directly below us on the second floor. I noticed that although our downstairs neighbors waved and smiled, they never spoke. I soon realized the reason: Victor and Helen Saggase were deaf. I couldn't help but be reminded of my father, who had been partially deaf.

The Saggases were about 10 years older than Frannie and me, but the four of us soon became good friends. Helen and Victor were a good-looking couple. They had a large circle of friends in the deaf community. By Christmas, Frannie and I were regularly invited to play checkers

▶ 1958 - Victor and Helen Saggase
Taught me sign language. Initially we communicated by writing notes, but soon Victor taught me to finger spell and I began to pick up sign.

and cards with them. Victor and I were both competitive, which led to serious battles at the game table. Initially, we communicated by writing notes or gesturing with our hands. Soon, though, I learned to finger spell and began to pick up a little sign language.

As graduation approached, I began to interview at various companies. Following my father's footsteps into the insurance business appealed to me. Four of my uncles – Rab and Frank Maguire, Frank Gaynor, and Jimmie Broderick – worked at Met Life and encouraged me to join the company.

▸ 1944 - Robert (Rab) Maguire, La Salle College

Rab, my father's youngest brother whose given name was Robert, was a basketball star at La Salle College in Philadelphia – his quickness on the court had earned him the nickname Rab, short for rabbit. At Met Life, he was a field-training instructor who became my mentor, and I listened to what he had to say. Frank Maguire, the third oldest of the Maguire brothers, and Frank Gaynor, who was married to my mother's sister, Helen, had gotten their jobs at Metropolitan Life through my father. Both had become district managers in Philadelphia. Jimmie Broderick, the husband of my father's sister, Kitty, started as a debit agent and held that sales position until he retired.

By the middle of May 1958, I applied for and was hired by Met Life as a sales agent in the company's Germantown district office, the same office where my father had started his career 30 years earlier. I knew that I would have to work doubly hard to uphold the family name. Even before I officially joined the company, scores of my father's friends and business associates reminded me that I would be traveling his same path. No such reminder was needed.

Deciding to follow in my father's footsteps simply made me more determined.

It wasn't that I felt nervous or inadequate. Rather, deciding to follow in my father's footsteps simply made me more determined to do whatever it took to prosper at Met Life. There was no way I would let Tom Maguire's son be anything but the best.

The encouragement of my uncles meant much to me, but Met Life's biggest attraction was the fact that I would be paid commissions on the policies I sold. I wanted my compensation to reflect my performance. The harder I worked, the more I made, and I planned on working very hard, indeed. I was on my way: determined to be known as more than Frannie McLaughlin's husband.

▶ **Brother Tom, Uncle Rab, and Jim**
Rab became my surrogate father after my father's death.

Happy, Sometimes Angry, and in a Hurry

Pleased as I was with my prospects, I still had not gained control of my Irish temper. Frannie and I had been married a little less than two years, so she had witnessed more than one of my outbursts – amazingly, she never complained. Something that always irritated me was seeing things out of place. One night I got angry when I stepped on several of Frannie's hairpins, which were scattered across the floor. She took it in stride – even after I slammed my fist against our eight inch television set, knocking it to the floor.

Most people would have reacted with anger, perhaps even walked out, but not Frannie. "Jimmy realized he'd done something stupid," she once explained, "especially when he realized we were without a television." (In my defense, I've always claimed I fell against the television.) But I must say that, over time, her serenity and calm response to my outbursts helped me to learn to control my temper.

In some ways, as I look back, I think my temper was triggered by my always being in a hurry to succeed – the impatience of youth exacerbated by the knowledge that I had already wasted a lot of time. I was always direct and with a bull-like determination. Sometimes, in building my business, the sheer force of my ambition pushed me beyond my limits. (As Eustace Wolfington has said more than once, "Jimmy would rather run through the wall than around it.")

▶ June 1958 - Graduation from Saint Joseph's University

In the background was the "cardboard college": Second World War barracks converted to classrooms. An emotional day for Frannie, me, and Fr. Hunter Guthrie – I had tears in my eyes.

I graduated from Saint Joseph's on June 8, 1958, earning a Bachelor of Science degree with the 3.0 grade point average I had promised Ruth. We were already seated as the faculty began to parade into the auditorium for the 11:00 A.M. graduation ceremony when I spotted Father Guthrie. Resplendent in his multicolored academic regalia, he broke from the procession when he saw me and walked to where I was seated. I stood up as he approached. I had tears in my eyes, and neither of us spoke as he hugged me.

After the ceremony, my family and friends, including Father Guthrie and the Saggases, joined Frannie and me at our apartment for what had to be a short celebration. I had to catch a 2:00 P.M. train to New York, where I was scheduled to begin two weeks of training at Met Life. Before I could earn my commission money, I had to earn my insurance license.

The next day, I wrote a thank-you note to my mother on Gramercy Park Hotel stationery. Although I called her Ruth in person, I addressed her as "My dearest Mother" in the letter. Just as I had written to her at the end of my stint in the Army, now I wanted to express my feelings at another important turning point in my life. To Ruth, I wrote:

Of course, words could never express my true gratitude, since I owe all I have ever in the slightest way attained to you. God will certainly say "job well done" to you. My college success will always be your secret victory since it was you, and you only, that made me realize my capability through your confidence in me and psychological handling of me in my deepest hours of despair. I shall always realize your important part in my first man-size accomplishment. You're so wonderful, Mom, and I love you so very much. Words could never in a million years express my deep love for you.

In a postscript, I added, "Must sign off... school is very hard, challenging. Have to put in several hours per night on homework."

I was working harder than I ever had before, preparing for what I thought of as my next "man-size accomplishment." I was determined to become every bit the man my father had been and more.

"Success is a journey"

James J. Maguire
Founder, Philadelphia Insurance Companies

Chapter 3
My Life at Met Life

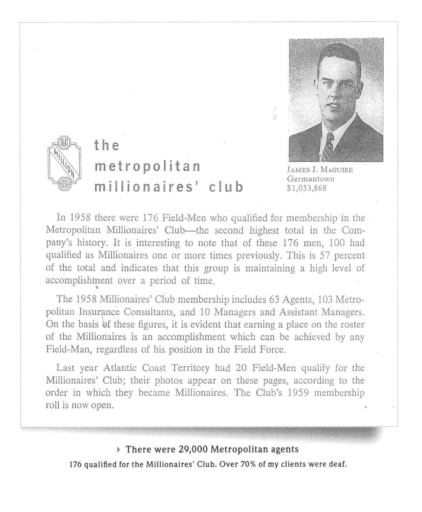

▸ There were 29,000 Metropolitan agents
176 qualified for the Millionaires' Club. Over 70% of my clients were deaf.

Long before I joined Met Life, I had come to rely on my Uncle Rab. In those first awful days after my father's death, he and his wife, Helen, provided me solace. They offered me a bed in their Philadelphia apartment and the use of their car. In later years, Frannie and I enjoyed many Sunday dinners at their house. But perhaps the most important thing Rab did for me was to help me identify my first niche in the insurance business.

Rab knew that Frannie and I had developed a friendship with the Saggases and that I was learning sign language. So before my first interview at Met Life, he made a suggestion: "Why

▸ Victor Saggase
My friend and sign language mentor.

don't you explain your connection with the deaf community and ask the underwriters at Met if they would consider issuing standard-rated policies to them?" If the underwriters agreed, the hearing impaired would pay the same rates as the hearing.

Victor Saggase had told me that there were upwards of 150 families living in the Delaware Valley who were hearing impaired. Many had children at the Pennsylvania School for the Deaf, so he felt confident that the market for such policies was substantial. After some discussion at the home office, Met Life agreed to test market my proposal – surely a first for a job applicant and definitely a first for the industry.

There were upwards of 150 families living in the Delaware Valley who were hearing impaired.

At the end of my two-week training session at Met Life headquarters, Cecil B. North, the man who had spoken so eloquently at my father's funeral, stood before our group and offered his wisdom. Then in his middle 50s, his red hair touched with gray, Cecil (I called him Mr. North in those days) was clearly a man on his way up. Indeed, he would take over as president of the company in November 1959. Imagine how I felt when he said, "Jim, would you join me up here?" Once again, he spoke fondly of my dad. Then he turned to me and asked, "How are you going to fill your father's shoes?"

"Mr. North," I replied, "the first thing I plan to do is qualify for the Million Dollar Roundtable."

Cecil smiled broadly. "You sound just like your father," he said.

The Roundtable is the company's most prestigious and competitive incentive program. It recognizes agents who sell more than a million dollars – face value – of insurance in a single year. In 1958, of 29,000 sales representatives in the United States, only 176 qualified.

The following Monday morning, having completed my training, I reported to the one-story building on Stenton Avenue that housed Met Life's Germantown office. In the front lobby was a reception area that held a few chairs and a coffee table. Ferns sat on tables in two corners. It was here that policyholders could come to pay their insurance premiums. There was a teller's window, much like a bank, where a young lady greeted customers. But the real action took place in the large bullpen that opened off of manager Bill McBride's office. Thirty-five metal desks were lined up to accommodate salespeople like me, along with a podium and blackboard from which Bill and his assistant managers held forth at our weekly Friday meetings.

At Met Life, salespeople were charged with "collecting their debit," which was a list of customers assigned by location. My original debit was a 12-block area in Glenside, Pennsylvania, a Philadelphia suburb. Every week, salespeople were responsible for calling on their customers, collecting premiums on in-force policies, and looking for opportunities to sell new policies. Perhaps a child had finished school and was starting a job, which created a need for life insurance. Or maybe a baby had been born and the parents needed to rethink the insurance needs of the breadwinner. On Friday morning, between 8 and 10:30 A.M., each salesman – there were no saleswomen in the office back then – turned in his collections for the week, listed any people behind in their payments, and reported new sales.

I arrived that first Monday morning eager to get started and more than eager to sell policies as fast as I could. Instead, like every other new salesman, I was handed a 100-page debit book, a binder with names and payment history. This was my Glenside debit, and my manager, Frank Pelleggi, was assigned to accompany me in the field for a week of training. Going from house to house, collecting weekly, monthly, and quarterly premiums, wasn't an onerous task. But from the start, I thought it was a waste of my time. I confided to Frank that I had a niche market with scores of potential customers already lined up. "I've got business I can bring in right now," I said.

Frank, a semi-pro football player who packed about 280 pounds on his five-foot, nine-inch frame, was my kind of guy. When I told him about my plan to market to the deaf community, he understood and was excited by the potential. So instead of dismissing me as an overeager newcomer, he encouraged me by offering to reassign the collections while I set about landing new accounts. Over the next two weeks, Frank collected the premiums on my Glenside debit while Victor and I called on the deaf community and sold 10 life insurance policies. At the time, the average agent sold one or two insurance contracts a month.

Frank was bowled over. Each week when I reported my sales, he would squeal with delight. "You're a phenom, Maguire!" he'd shriek. When the national numbers first came out, he would rush to my desk. "Suck it up, baby," he would razz me, "you're only 19th from first place!" I was driven, and nothing was going to stop me from qualifying for the Million Dollar Roundtable.

From time to time on Sundays, the Saggases would drive 10 miles or so to Camden, New Jersey, just across the Delaware River. There, they would attend a church that ministered to the deaf. The entire service was conducted in sign language. One Sunday, Victor invited Frannie and me to go with them. "I have a lot of people who want to meet you," he said. "Be prepared to stick around after the service." I wasn't convinced that I'd actually sell any policies that day, but I brought my briefcase, rate book, and applications just in case. I thought I'd meet some deaf people and, with any luck, call on them later.

We sat next to Victor and Helen in the first row. When the minister began his sermon by introducing me and Frannie, I was taken by surprise. "Jim Maguire is in the congregation today," he said, explaining that I was a Metropolitan Life insurance consultant who had prevailed upon the company to underwrite coverage for the hearing impaired at standard rates. No company in the industry does that for the deaf, he said. He paused before saying that the congregation was welcome to meet with me following the service.

Victor poked me and signaled for me to stand up. When I turned to face the congregation, all hands were gently shaking above their heads, the sign for clapping.

That afternoon, Victor introduced me to more than three dozen families, and we compiled a list of more than 50 likely customers from among the people I had briefly met. By 4 P.M. that day, I had filled out eight applications and promised to contact others I didn't have time to interview. For the next two months, my evenings were spent following up with these people.

It wasn't long before my colleagues at Met Life started wondering what I was up to. There never was any announcement by Met about standard rates for the deaf, so my secret market was truly a secret. Jimmie McNutt, a cranky old assistant manager who had known my father, was especially leery of my numbers. But Frank never let slip any word of my niche. By the beginning of my third month, I had a steady flow of prospects culled from referrals passed by one deaf client to another.

Frannie and I made sure we reciprocated. Whether we needed to have our shoes repaired, our clothes cleaned, or our furniture re-upholstered, we tried to patronize businesses owned by the hearing impaired. And on two separate occasions, Victor asked me to accompany a deaf friend to a minor court hearing. Back then, long before the 1990 passage of the Americans with Disabilities Act, there were few certified sign-language interpreters. I wasn't fluent in sign language by any means, but I could tell a hearing impaired person what was being said.

A funny incident took place when Frannie and I were on a Saturday picnic at an amusement park with a group of deaf couples and their children. On our way home we stopped to get something to eat. Everybody was signing as we sat down. When one of the waitresses commented to another that "it's going to be fun taking this order," I piped up saying, "I'll help you." It stopped her cold in her tracks.

When I told Cecil North that I was setting my sights on qualifying for the Million Dollar Roundtable, I'm sure that neither he nor anyone else in the room expected me to do it. Why would they? I hadn't even begun selling for the company until the last week in June of 1958. That meant I had less than 20 weeks to qualify. But I flabbergasted everyone by making the grade within 13 weeks. Seventy percent of my policies were sold to deaf clients.

The celebration for the "Millionaires" was held in April 1959. The site was the Boca Raton Club in Boca Raton, Florida. On April 28, the *Germantown Courier* ran an article announcing that I was among "the 176 leaders [out] of almost 29,000 Metropolitan field representatives in the United States and Canada." Next to the article was a picture of me and "Mrs. Maguire" at the celebration. The paper didn't say so, but Mrs. Maguire and I, frugal as ever, had endured a 22-hour car ride from Philadelphia to Boca Raton in my Chevy.

▶ **Frannie and Jim in Boca Raton, Florida**
Mr. Maguire takes part in a four-day business conference with the sales leaders of Metropolitan Life Insurance Company.

Among the youngest in attendance, Frannie and I sometimes felt overwhelmed. Excited and nervous at the start, I became tongue-tied on two occasions. The first was when Cecil North stepped onto the elevator as we were going down from our hotel room for the welcoming cocktail and dinner party. It was an elaborate affair held in a ballroom awash with ice sculptures, lavish table settings, and a bustling crew of black-tied and white-gloved waiters. "I'm eager to hear your presentation tomorrow," North said. Trying to exude confidence, I smiled and said, "Stand by, it's a good one!"

The story of my success in the deaf community was out and I was invited to participate in a marketing roundtable. Suddenly, I was being touted as a marketing wunderkind. But the high point of the day came just before my presentation when Cecil introduced me as "Tommy Maguire's son, one of Met Life's greatest executives."

Suddenly, I was being touted as a marketing wunderkind.

It was an emotional moment for me. When I stood to speak, I felt my knees buckle and beads of perspiration pop out on my forehead. I had spent time preparing in front of a mirror, but now I couldn't remember what I planned to say. After stumbling through some opening words from my written text and losing my place, I finally stopped reading and spoke from my heart. I took a deep breath and explained how Met Life had become a champion to the hearing impaired by being the first in the industry to insure my deaf clients with standard rates. I told of Frank Pelleggi excusing me from debit collection and picking up premium payments for me.

▶ When I qualified for the Roundtable for the second time, only 50% of my sales were to the deaf community.

I had given away my sales secret, but my success story was rightfully shared by Frank, who believed in me, and by Met Life, which had the foresight and courage to buck industry standards and charge the hearing impaired standard rates.

Frannie had a wonderful time. Her only complaint was that I insisted on leaving on Sunday afternoon so that I could get back by Tuesday morning. We drove all night and all day Monday, but I was eager to get started on my new goal: I intended to qualify for the roundtable two years in a row.

Now that my niche market was out in the open, however, I realized that competition would not be far behind. Salesmen from other companies, as well as within Met Life, began to target the hearing impaired. One Met Life salesman was the hearing son of deaf parents in Elizabeth, New Jersey, and he began working the north Jersey and New York market. Unlike me, he was fluent in sign language.

I finally stopped reading and spoke from my heart.

Strictly on My Own

In 1959, I was again the first to qualify for the Roundtable, thus becoming its youngest president. This time, though, it took me eight months and two days to do it, and only 50 percent of my policies were sold to the deaf. I had been in the insurance business less than two years, but I had already learned an important lesson: You can't hold onto a profitable niche forever. Once you find one, start preparing for the day you may lose it. Recognizing that there were only a finite number of hearing-impaired prospects in the Delaware Valley, I started calling on the business community in search of my next niche. I put in an enormous number of hours. My days were spent prospecting for new business customers, and my evenings were taken up with selling to and serving my deaf clients.

Increasingly, standard policies were being sold to the deaf community, and I was happy for that. But as a life insurance salesman, I was frustrated that I wasn't able to offer a full line of insurance products. Several of my clients – the Philadelphia Pen & Paper Company, a printing business, several auto dealerships, and a pharmacy, among others – had asked me to handle all of their insurance needs. Unsure about what I should do, I once again turned to Uncle Rab for advice.

▶ **The Rab and Helen Maguire Family**
Eileen, Susan, Dianne, Debbie and Jennifer.
He told me: "Go to work for yourself."

"I'm thinking about leaving Met Life and starting my own agency," I told him. I went on to explain that, alternatively, I might consider forming an alliance with a local property-and-casualty agency and working with both it and Met Life. Rab wasn't a fan of the alliance idea. "It's like having one foot in the boat and one on the pier," he said.

Like me, Rab was athletic, and he and I enjoyed running together on Saturday mornings. After one such run, we talked about my career and he flat out told me I should leave Met Life. "You've got the education, personality, and sales talent to build your own insurance business," he told me. "If you don't get out now while you're young, you may never leave. The fact is, you're not going to get rich with Metropolitan, but you could make a killing in property and casualty. Go to work for yourself." After a brief pause, he confided that he regretted not having done the same thing himself.

I had been in the insurance business less than two years, but I had already learned an important lesson: You can't hold onto a profitable niche forever. Once you find one, start preparing for the day you may lose it.

As I might have predicted, my Uncle Frank Gaynor couldn't imagine how I could even consider breaking from "Mother Met." "You'll never make it in business on your own," he stated flatly. "You'll be back at Met Life within a year." Frank never knew it, but that comment alone made me more determined to succeed than anything anyone else did or said. He always believed that it was Met Life, not me, that was responsible for my success. I may have identified the deaf market, but it was the company that decided to underwrite the hearing impaired at standard rates. Frank was a good man, but he was very much a company man. I knew I had the wherewithal to break from that mold.

When I told Frannie about my conversations with both Rab and Frank, she sided squarely with Rab. It was about this time that Frannie told me she was expecting our first child. Under the circumstances, no one would have blamed her for worrying about our financial security. Yet Frannie believed in me so strongly that my taking such a risk motivated her, which in turn motivated me. She knew that, at least for the next few months, we could continue building our savings with the money she made working for Dr. Harris. And I knew that my contract with Met Life guaranteed policy-renewal commissions for a full year.

Ruth, like Frannie, liked the idea of me striking out on my own. "You'll make a go of it," she said, "I'm sure of it."

"You'll never make it in business on your own," he stated flatly.

At the end of November 1959, I submitted my resignation to Met Life. Hoping to keep me, the company sent Ernie Beckley, the vice president of the Atlantic coast territory, down to Germantown to offer me more money and additional incentives. But my mind was made up.

The week before I left, Cecil North, now president of Met, called to congratulate me on qualifying again for the Million Dollar Roundtable. Gracious as always, he told me, "I respect your decision."

▶ **November 1959**
Exiting Met Life

On my last day, I had lunch with Bill McBride and Frank Pelleggi. I thanked both of them for their support. My departure that day marked not an end, but the beginning of a new professional life.

"Motivated people make America great"

James J. Maguire
Founder, Philadelphia Insurance Companies

Chapter 4
On My Own

▸ Jamie - May 1960
No amount of pride over anything I ever accomplished could top what I felt.

I had been in the insurance business all of 18 months. I had a wife, a baby on the way, and not much money in the bank. Still, I decided to go into business for myself. "Starting a business," best-selling author Seth Godin once wrote, "is far easier than making it successful." I would find that out, but not until later.

At the time, I wasn't looking for a mentor, but one appeared in the person of Lee Waggoner. Lee was president of the life insurance unit of the Philadelphia-based Insurance Company of North America (INA). He had recently been hired to revitalize INA's weak life insurance operation and was casting around in Philadelphia for new talent. I had been written up as a life insurance success story so when he heard that I was starting my own agency to sell property and casualty insurance, he invited me to come and see him.

When I walked into his office, Lee – a handsome, impeccably groomed man with a hint of a southern accent – extended his hand. He talked and acted like someone accustomed to accomplishing whatever he sets out to do.

"How would you like to go to the INA property-casualty school?" he asked.

I accepted without hesitation, knowing the program was one of the best in the country. The next 10-week session was set to begin in January 1960. There was just one hitch: The INA program trained only INA agents, so, technically, I wasn't eligible. Never one to let a technicality stand in his way, Lee picked up the phone and dialed the program director, Joe Young.

"Joe," he said, "enroll Jim Maguire in the next INA course." The quid pro quo? I would sell INA life products when I got my agency off the ground.

The INA classes were intense. They started at 8:45 A.M. and ran until 4:30 P.M., breaking only for lunch. Poor performance could get you booted out. To cope, we helped each other. Most days after class we got together to study and sweat over our homework, much like the study groups I had organized in my Saint Joe's days.

I completed the program in early April and wasted no time in applying to the Pennsylvania Insurance Department to sit for the state examination in Harrisburg. The almost three-week wait seemed interminable. The examination itself was a three-hour ordeal, with both multiple-choice and essay questions that probed my knowledge of workers' compensation, auto and property insurance, and more. I knew I had done well, but in those days, tests were graded by hand, leaving me in the dark about my score until early May. The letter announcing I had passed came with a license application to be filled out and returned with a $25 check. More weeks went by before I finally received my license.

All told, five months elapsed from the day I began the INA course to the day I actually had my property-casualty license. But I wasn't idle. I spent part of the time selling life insurance for INA from a desk and phone the company provided. Now, with license in hand, I could open my own office and get started building the Maguire Agency.

My very pregnant Frannie found time that spring to help me locate and decorate an office. I signed a lease, effective May 1, 1960, for a 400-square-foot walk-up on the second floor of 156 West Chelten Avenue in Germantown. I paid all of $300 a month. We were above a bakery and shared the second floor with a travel agency and a one-man law firm.

Lee Waggoner gave me a filing cabinet and two metal desks, which sat on either side of the glass front door. I bought a typewriter and secondhand straight-back chairs that I positioned next to the desks. A 10- by 15-foot red Oriental rug that Frannie picked up at a garage sale covered the floor. The office had one big drawback — no windows. Frannie's solution was to sew floor-length drapes that we hung along the entire back wall, giving the illusion of a nice, large window.

May 1, 1960

JAMES J. MAGUIRE

formerly with Metropolitan Life Insurance Co.

announces the opening of the Maguire Insurance Agency

located at 156 West Chelten Avenue, Philadelphia 44, Pa.

consultation in all lines of insurance is available

Telephone
VI 8-1200
WA 4-1946

▸ **May 1960**

My favorite part of the office, though, was the front door. There, in gold leaf, it read:

JAMES J MAGUIRE
CONSULTANT
MAGUIRE INSURANCE AGENCY

I purchased stationery and business cards telling the world that the Maguire Insurance Agency was run by James J. Maguire, President.

If I needed any further impetus to succeed it arrived on May 6, 1960, with the birth of our first child. I had driven Frannie to the hospital around 10:00 P.M. the night before, got her checked in, and then went home and crawled into bed. That's what fathers-to-be did in the '60s. At 6:30 the next morning, the phone rang. "It's a boy," the obstetrician announced.

No amount of pride over anything I'd ever accomplished could top the chest-swelling I felt the first time I saw James J. Maguire, Jr. We called him Jamie from the start. He weighed in at 6 pounds, 10 ounces, and was 20 inches long, with fair skin, blond hair, and blue eyes. From day one, Jamie had a pleasant disposition. He was such a good sleeper and so content that he didn't bother to walk until he was almost 15 months old. Who could have guessed that this placid little boy dozing through the grand opening of the agency would one day become CEO of the Philadelphia Insurance Companies?

About a month after the June 15th grand opening, and less than two months after Jamie's birth, Frannie was back working in the office for three or four hours a day. We set up a white bassinet for Jamie, who never lacked for attention no matter how busy we were. Our second-floor office neighbors, Mary Jo and Mike Concannon in the travel agency and Herman Sunheim in the law office, dropped in regularly to see the baby. Herman, who perpetually wore a bow tie and seersucker suit, was eager for me to succeed, especially now that we had Jamie. He was kind enough to refer a number of clients to me.

Referrals were appreciated, but making sales proved a challenge. I found myself calling on anyone and everyone. The property and casualty business was more complex than life insurance. I had to consider types of liability exposure, previous experience, adequate loss controls, competitors' willingness to compromise underwriting, and pricing. I liked the challenge, but I still had a lot to learn.

My affiliation with INA and the relationship with Lee Waggoner proved to be an enormous advantage because it set me apart from other agents. INA at the time was considered to be one of the premier companies in the industry and Lee Waggoner had a lot of clout — especially if you were producing life business. I still needed every lead I could get. To build my portfolio of life accounts outside the deaf community, I again decided to specialize by gathering new birth records from Philadelphia hospitals. I would then contact the families to set up evening sales appointments.

During the day, I identified certain markets and made cold calls. I loved to walk into a small business and ask to see the general manager or owner. Good at getting past the front desk, I regularly managed to see the people who could make insurance decisions. I cold-called printing companies, drugstores, body-repair shops, bakeries, auto dealers, and more.

From the beginning, I believed that offering a better product, not necessarily a lower price, was the key to success. My association with a well-known company like INA was an invaluable calling card. But I wasn't content just to hold onto someone else's coattails. I wanted to set myself apart in other ways, too. Based on what I had learned from my cold calls with local businesses, I designed an underwriting survey. The questions and answers allowed me to assess the insurance needs of prospective customers. I presented myself as a consultant gathering pertinent information. By shedding my salesman's mantle, I did some of the best selling of my life.

Each customer presented his or her own particular challenges – but none was trickier or harder to land than a car dealership owned by Eustace Wolfington. I was initially attracted to the account because it was the first dealership in the area offering customers the option of leasing rather than purchasing a car. "Try before you buy" was their marketing slogan. Customers could lease an auto for two years and if they liked it, they had the option to buy it at the depreciated value or return it and walk away. I had begun concentrating on auto dealers for two reasons:

1. The accounts were larger and the dealers tended to be entrepreneurial and likable.

2. INA was favorably disposed to offering competitive terms and coverage.

▸ **Eustace Wolfington (center right) donating a Chevrolet in 1965**
Landing the Wolfington Dealership account was a tough challenge.

Although Eustace and I knew each other from our days at Saint Joseph's University, we were not particularly close friends. When I offered to conduct an audit of his company's insurance needs, he gave me the runaround: "A friend handles our insurance . . . I'm happy with his price and coverage . . . I don't have time for a survey . . . I'll get back to you" were some of his excuses.

I concentrated first on getting Eustace to let me conduct an audit. In an offhand manner, I asked if his garage liability contract included coverage when he or his wife drove someone else's car. As a matter of fact, it did not. My foot was in the door. The more questions I asked, the more holes I found in his existing program. In the end, I not only won Eustace's account, it opened the door to a 50-year-and-counting friendship.

Breaking New Ground

By the summer of 1961, the agency was growing, and I needed more help than Frannie could provide. I asked Connie Byrne, my former accounting professor at Saint Joe's, to come in every three months to help me prepare quarterly financial statements. Connie wouldn't let me pay him at first, but I insisted: he was invaluable in setting up my bookkeeping system. Soon I hired a full-time assistant and a part-time bookkeeper. Now I was free to spend more of my time doing what I did best – sell insurance.

▶ **Connie Byrne**
Accounting professor, Saint Joseph's University, and independent auditor for my company in the early 1960s.

In the end, I not only won Eustace's account, it opened the door to a 50-year-and-counting friendship.

I loved being my own boss. In 1963, while trying to sign up small- to medium-sized business accounts, I developed the concept of premium finance. I asked Marshall Delametter, the manager of a Philadelphia National Bank branch near my office, to finance the premiums. He wasn't interested but he did introduce me to Leon Krause, the owner of the Raleigh Loan Company, a small, Pennsylvania-licensed consumer lender. Before long, Leon and I were in acquisition talks, and when the deal was struck, I didn't have to clear it with anyone – I just did it.

At the time, insurance companies required commercial accounts to pay a substantial part of the annual premium at the contract's inception. By offering business clients the option of paying in 10 equal monthly installments, I gained a competitive edge. If an account was large enough or if there was competition, I offered a low-interest line of credit as well.

My first borrower was a dry cleaner who needed $10,000 to purchase equipment. Soon, word of mouth was bringing more small Philadelphia businessmen to Raleigh's lending window, and we were making $10,000 to $25,000 loans.

I had created a new niche business, though not all of my accounts proved to be good borrowers. In my eagerness to write insurance, I sometimes made poor decisions about loans, and chasing monthly payments was costing me money and time. I needed a tough collection agent. My 57-year-old mother, who kept such careful accounts of our paper routes and bike loans as youngsters, was perfect for the job.

▶ 1964 - Ruth Maguire
When Ruth called, customers knew they had to pay.

The "Family" Business Expands

Ruth was terrific when it came to collecting receivables, spurred on, in part, by having a stake in the outcome. When I bought Raleigh Loan, Ruth mortgaged her house to give me the down payment I needed. From that day on, she did everything she could to make sure our borrowers paid what was due and on time. When Ruth called, customers knew they had to pay up or lose their coverage, and I'd often tell customers, only half-jokingly, "I'll check with Ruth!"

▶ Ruth (front left), Arlette (back left),
Nancy (back right), Joe Werner (office)1965

Eustace, who was truly fond of my mother, says that "if you had two bills that needed to be paid and you had to choose, the first one you paid was the one you owed Maguire Agency. You didn't dare risk a call from Ruth – or worse, the look she would give you if you walked into the office."

I hired a full-time bookkeeper, Arlette Chellis, in 1964. Arlette, who had previously been employed by a small accounting firm, was a 35-year-old Philadelphia native, a Temple University graduate, and an African American.

▶ 1964 - Arlette Chellis and Jim

Equal rights for blacks in the '60s was a national issue. I hired Arlette, however, not only for her qualifications and capabilities but to demonstrate our commitment to being an equal opportunity employer. She quickly threw herself into the job and became a close friend to Ruth, Frannie, and me. I was grateful and lucky that she came to work for my company.

A New Lease on Leasing

I've always been happy to do business with friends based on nothing more than a handshake. And there is no friend I trust more than Eustace Wolfington.

We both came from large families and lost our fathers early – mine was 45 and Eustace's was 47. In his younger days, Eustace wanted a career in the hotel industry. He traveled to New York as often as he could to visit Conrad Hilton, the legendary hotelier, to familiarize himself with the business. But when his widowed mother was left with nine children and part-ownership in a family-founded car dealership dating back two generations, Eustace put aside his dreams and went to work at the dealership. Like me, he was not content to be "just a salesman" and quickly began to develop innovative ways to make it easier and more affordable for people to drive new cars.

Car leasing to consumers was a new concept in the 1960s. Until then, the only way a consumer could get a new car was to buy it. With the advent of leasing, a customer could drive a new car for two or three years and then return it to the dealer at the end of the lease. Eustace enthusiastically embraced the new concept and it got me thinking.

I approached INA with the idea of providing insurance to the lessee. I wanted the dealer to include the coverage and cost in the lease contract. The dealer would then send me the monthly premium, which I would forward, minus my commission, to INA. Naturally, Eustace was one of the first people I pitched on this concept.

Eustace wasn't sold on including insurance until I explained that, as the titled owner of the vehicle, he would be held liable in the event of an accident if the lessee wasn't insured or failed to maintain adequate coverage. Eustace didn't need any more convincing.

It was the Wolfington Chevrolet leasing account that turned the ignition switch on what would become a very lucrative market that eventually catapulted me to national prominence.

Joy and Pain at Blue Bell

The company was growing, and so was our family. Susan, whom we called Susie, was born on Father's Day, June 18, 1961. A beautiful, blue-eyed blonde, our first daughter was perpetually happy and showed it with her infectious smile. Unlike her placid brother, Susie was a bundle of energy. At 11 months, she was up and running.

▶ 1964 - Susie, Jamie, and David Confer
David became part of our family and remained with us for two years.

Within a few months, Frannie was pregnant again, prompting us to put our three-bedroom home on the market. We needed more space, both inside and out. The agency was prospering, so we felt secure enough to buy a four-bedroom, split-level in the Philadelphia suburb of Blue Bell.

We moved in March of 1962 and immediately fell in love with our new home. Set on an acre of land, the house had a fireplace, a family room, and enough space to accommodate our growing family. The first summer there I had the kids in an inflatable wading pool in the backyard. My new neighbor called over in jest to compliment me on my fine pool. That's all I needed! That afternoon I called a pool company who came out and built a 20-by-40-foot swimming pool that quickly became our family entertainment center.

Frannie's third pregnancy was a difficult one, and her doctor ordered hospital bed rest for the final two months. Nevertheless, she went into labor prematurely on May 10, 1962. When I came to visit her at the hospital a few minutes after 7:00 P.M., as was my custom, I met with a chaotic and frightening situation. Frannie had gone through the delivery alone. The nurses were changing shifts and either missed or ignored her calls for help.

Our second son weighed just 2 pounds. Named Edward Thomas after our fathers, he lived only three days. We mourned his loss for a very long time and still regularly visit his grave. Despite our sadness, we knew we were blessed to have Jamie and Susie, and we did our best to carry on.

Six months later and still grieving, we took in a three-year-old foster child from Saint Mary's orphanage. His birth mother unable to care for him, David Confer became part of our family and remained with us for two years. David brought joy to our family that helped us through that difficult time. To this day we often talk about David and pray that he's okay and that our short life together had a positive effect on his life.

"To thine own self be true"

William Shakespeare

Chapter 5
From Rough Roads to the Fast Lane

▶ 1965 - I purchased an abandoned A&P supermarket

As much as we savored the warm and yeasty aromas that wafted up from the bakery below, it was time for the Maguire Agency to find new space. As was our family, our business was growing rapidly, and we had been forced to lease a separate office down the hall to accommodate bookkeeping and policy renewals. The new arrangement was neither cozy nor efficient and prevented me from adding more people. So when the opportunity arose at the end of 1964 to purchase an abandoned A&P supermarket just a few blocks away, I simply couldn't pass it up. I paid $40,000 for the property and approximately $40,000 to gut the space and convert it to offices.

The one-story, rectangular building had a 12-foot ceiling and 4,800 square feet of floor space, more than 10 times the space of the West Chelten office and certainly more than we needed at that point. In my typical take-charge fashion, I never even considered hiring an architect. Instead, I called one of my clients, a local general contractor, Johnnie Coraluzzi, and sat down with him to lay out the offices.

Inside, we installed a 10-foot dropped acoustical ceiling, and to give the exterior a colonial look, a bow window was placed on either side of the center entrance. The lobby was furnished with armchairs, a coffee table, and side tables with lamps – all of it sectioned off from the office space by a 50-inch-high white picket fence. An open work area behind the fence contained six desks, and behind that was a center hall lined with six spacious private offices. A large, glass-enclosed, gold-leaf sign in the lobby area proclaimed:

MAGUIRE INSURANCE AGENCY INC
INSURANCE CONSULTANTS

This time, Frannie didn't have to turn to her sewing machine to camouflage a wall without windows. With 60 feet of street frontage, the new offices got plenty of natural light. We moved

▶ 1965 - New building, Chelten Avenue West

in the week before Thanksgiving in 1965, and celebrated our grand opening by inviting members from the Germantown Businessmen's Association to a wine and cheese party.

My euphoria was diminished somewhat, however, by a falling-out I had with my friend and early supporter at INA, Lee Waggoner. When he learned that the American Casualty Insurance Company was getting half my life insurance business, he was not happy. American Casualty was paying me a substantially higher commission than INA and, as an independent operator, I felt that I should do what was best for my company. As a result, tensions between Lee and me flared. Despite my arrangement with American Casualty, I continued to honor my commitment to INA by giving them half of my life insurance production.

Nevertheless, Lee was mad as hell and sent a truck to pick up the two desks and file cabinet he had given me four and a half years earlier. I was upset that he was angry and quickly contacted him to make peace. Lee eventually understood that I did not want to be a captive agent and he calmed down. Our business relationship went on as before and we continued to be friends.

Tough Breaks

Even if Frannie had wanted to make drapes for the new offices, she was hardly in a position to do so. Christopher, a beautiful and mild-tempered boy, made his debut on February 16, 1965, joining brother Jamie and sister Susie in the Blue Bell nursery. Christopher was chubbier than his siblings, weighing in at 9 pounds, 14 ounces on a 22-inch frame. He was such a good baby that we hardly knew he was in the house.

Frannie – only 29 when Chris was born – had always been active, athletic, and outgoing. Among her achievements was winning the 50-yard dash in the eighth grade at the prestigious Penn Relays. But with three children under the age of five and an Irish setter vying for her time, she found it harder to pursue the outdoor activities she enjoyed so much.

When Chris was two months old, we decided to get away for a three-day weekend of skiing without the children. We left them with a relative, Sabina Cavanaugh, who was married to a second cousin of Frannie's father. Then we took off for Elk Mountain. The Union Dale ski resort was about a two-and-a-half-hour drive north of Philadelphia. Located in the Poconos, Elk Mountain's trails are among the best in Pennsylvania and most of the runs there are challenging and for advanced skiers.

Since our marriage in November 1957, vacations had been few and far between, what with the crush of a new and expanding business and the demands of the children. We were excited to be getting away for what felt like a mini-honeymoon. We arrived on a Friday looking forward to a whole weekend together without interruptions.

The bliss was short-lived. Our first day on the slopes, barely an hour after we arrived, Frannie fell and shattered her left fibula when her boot did not release from the ski. I'll never forget seeing her foot pointing backward, still locked into the ski. We found out later that the slopes had been closed because of heavy icing just after we jumped off the ski lift and started on our first run, which made it almost impossible to get Frannie off the slope after her fall.

Unable to get a snowmobile up the icy slope, the ski patrol had to restart the ski lift to get up the mountain and with a sled stretcher in hand, they skied down to where Frannie lay in the snow and carried her to safety.

Leaving my car at Elk Mountain, I rode with Frannie in a seemingly endless three-and-a-half-hour ambulance ride to suburban Philadelphia. Frannie's broken leg was wrapped in nothing more than an ace bandage, and every bump in the road was excruciatingly painful.

After her foot had been returned to the proper position and her leg encased in a cast, Frannie spent a full week in Holy Redeemer Hospital, followed by four weeks in bed at home and two more surgeries to graft bone from her hip and insert four pins. It would be a year before she could walk without a cast and crutches. And since the Blue Bell house was a split-level, I had to carry her up to the bedroom each night and back down in the morning.

Because Frannie was not ambulatory, I also took over Christopher's middle-of-the-night feedings. I still remember our late-night rendezvous as some of the most peaceful moments of fatherhood and have jokingly attributed Chris's placid disposition to my

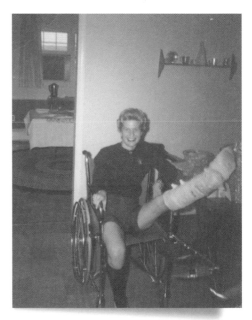

▶ **Frannie broke her leg skiing**
I rode with Frannie from Elk Mountain on a seemingly endless three-and-a-half-hour ambulance ride.

gentle touch. (Lord knows, in the years that followed whatever gentle touch I displayed then was displaced by stern discipline, when Chris might have preferred a gentler touch.)

The months when Frannie was out of commission were among the most challenging of our lives, but we got through them with the help of God, our families, and our friends.

> ## *The months when Frannie was out of commission were among the most challenging of our lives...*

Not every burden can be lightened, as when Frannie returned to Holy Redeemer in the late fall of 1965 to have the pins in her leg removed. Knowing that she was pregnant with our fifth child, she would not allow the doctors to sedate her. I was there when her doctor began the procedure. With only local anesthesia, which didn't seem to do much, Frannie repeatedly cried out. Seeing her suffer was too much for me and without warning I passed out and hit the tile floor with a thud. Suddenly, I was the center of attention, and Frannie promptly decided that the procedure should be postponed.

The plan was to remove the pins after Tim was born. Upon further examination, however, it was evident that the bone and pins were so closely bound that there was no reason to remove them. To this day, Frannie carries hardware in her left leg.

Adversity Strikes Again

In the summer of 1966, our prayers veered from thankfulness to sheer fright over the health of six-year-old Jamie. Frannie was making her usual morning rounds to check on each of our waking children when she discovered that Jamie was burning with fever. We called our friend and family physician, Jack Donald. He arrived within the hour and immediately determined that Jamie's temperature was 104 degrees. Jack scooped him up and plunged him into a tub of ice-cold water. Then, with Jack following close behind, we rushed Jamie to Chestnut Hill Hospital, where he was diagnosed with both encephalitis and meningitis. The condition, known as meningoencephalitis, is transmitted by the measles virus and is life threatening but not contagious. Five very tense days elapsed before Jamie started to improve, and he didn't come home for 10 days after that.

Seeing Red in 1967

Tim arrived on April 1, 1966, number five in the lineup. Because he was in a breech position, Frannie's labor lasted for 17 long hours. Thankfully, Tim was a healthy seven-pound, 20-inch towheaded addition to our family. Placid like his brother, Chris, Tim seldom cried – until, that is, the competition and companionship between the two boys began to emerge.

It's no secret that I love a challenge, and 1967 brought more than one. It was a volatile year in the insurance industry. "Redlining" had become a hot-button issue in Philadelphia and other major U.S. cities. As defined by the National Commission on Urban Problems, redlining is "a tacit agreement among all groups – specifically lending institutions and insurance companies – to block off certain areas within 'red lines' and not to loan or insure them." This was the insurance companies' heavy-handed attempt to rid themselves of worrisome ethnic and geographic exposure. The tactic, however, soon provoked a major governmental crackdown. The Pennsylvania Insurance Department passed regulations forbidding "place-based discrimination." The result was the outlawing of the cancellation of coverage simply because of the insured's property location. But before the regulations took effect, insurance companies had already jettisoned numerous policyholders.

For many insurance companies, however, the issue was more about survival than discrimination. Urban rioting, white flight, and the abandonment and destruction of property were inflicting heavy financial losses. After redlining was prohibited, insurance companies came up with another solution. They initiated a systematic plan to sever their relationships with agencies that wrote policies on city homes, businesses, or automobiles.

In the stable suburban neighborhoods where insurance companies hoped to find new business, they encountered aggressive competitors trying to muscle their way into the market. Making the situation worse, sophisticated insureds were becoming more litigious and lawyers were starting to sue insurance companies for pain and suffering. In short, the insurance industry was being buffeted by what I thought of as an industrial revolution. The comfort zone that existed during the 1950s was gone for good.

The Maguire Insurance Agency was not immune to the problems. One summer day, Joe Dugan, the Ohio Casualty representative with whom I did a lot of business, walked into my office and summarily announced that the company was pulling out of the Philadelphia market. I had 30 days to move my accounts. Given that Dugan had badgered me for two years to broker business to Ohio Casualty and stopped in regularly to ask for still more, my famous temper flared – I was mad as hell to be dropped like a hot potato without warning. Once I calmed down, I came to grips with the reality of the situation: I had a book of business that had to be moved without delay.

I quickly contacted the Hartford Insurance Company, which I had begun representing in conjunction with my car-leasing business. The Hartford reviewed my Ohio Casualty accounts, accepting or rejecting each one based on its merits. I had a solid relationship with Joe Achiavati, the Hartford's Philadelphia field representative. Joe saw the industry's problems as an opportunity. He liked my aggressive style, which no doubt influenced the company's decision to take over about 65 percent of my Ohio Casualty accounts. Unfortunately, the remaining 35 percent – largely customers with personal auto accounts – had to find their own replacement insurance.

As one problem was solved, another arose. I had started my business in 1960 with a salesman's mentality. I thought all I needed was someone to buy what I was selling. Now I was beginning to understand the importance of selecting customers based on their past insurance history. The Reliance Insurance Company, one of the companies I represented, thought it was high time I take action and deliver an ultimatum: Either recruit someone with underwriting know-how or our relationship was over.

I hired Ken Wilcutts, who was just slightly older than me. He was smart, well-organized, responsible, and possessed solid underwriting acumen. I came to depend heavily on him, and he helped me develop much better risk-selection procedures.

Even though the industry was in meltdown, our business was growing nicely so I decided in 1968 to put Raleigh Loan on the auction block. I needed to rid myself of peripheral distractions. In addition, there were disputes over the interest I charged and slow paybacks by some borrowers. All in all, the headaches outweighed the benefits.

The Equitable Loan Company snapped up Raleigh, paying $180,000, so I got Ruth's

▸ Kenneth J. Wilcutts, V.P.

$25,000 capital back plus a nice profit. Equitable agreed to open a one-man office in my building to continue servicing my accounts.

The agency continued to grow during the late '60s, an extremely volatile period in the insurance industry. It was a tough time, but I loved what I was doing and my attitude was always positive. There were great moments that I still treasure. One of the best occurred on a sunny day in

▸ **Muhammad Ali**

June of 1968. I often took Ruth and Arlette to Imhoffs restaurant on Friday for lunch. On one occasion, coming from the restaurant I spotted Muhammad Ali walking with another man along Chelten Avenue, just across the street. I shouted a big hello and Arlette and I bounded across the street in the middle of the block.

I had followed Ali's career from the beginning and respected him as much for his refusal to be drafted into the Vietnam War on religious grounds as for his boxing talent. Saint Joe's had taught me… "To thine own self be true," and Ali was living this belief. After defending his championship nine times in two years, he was stripped of his heavyweight title for sticking to his principles.

As we approached Ali, I could see the surprise on his face that my companion was an attractive young black girl. I stuck out my hand, introduced myself, and introduced Arlette as the CFO of our insurance agency. He was good looking, big, and outgoing with a great smile and I told him how good he looked and how much I admired him. I said the Vietnam War, in my opinion, was a bad deal. The encounter lasted about five minutes. The conversation ended with me telling Ali to stay in shape for the day he would re-enter the ring.

There is no way the champ could have known the pleasure I received from that encounter. He represented what I admired and everything my father taught me – independence, courage, physical fitness, pride, confidence. In my mind, I could draw a parallel between how I was living my life – being my own boss, staying physically fit, answering to no one – with the way Ali had performed in and out of the ring.

6 Steps *To Success*

1

Show up every day. Set goals and have dreams … Success is a marathon

"The will to win and reach your goal is not nearly as important as the will to prepare to win!"

2

Be passionate and positive about your dream … If you don't love it – you'll never make it.

"You must believe what you are and become what you believe"

3

Be a high achiever – In business that means being professional – You and you alone know if you're
giving a full measure of your effort.

"To thine own self be true." –William Shakespeare

4

To be successful … You have to stay fit physically and mentally / stay positive / stay motivated …

"Motivated people make America great!"

5

The most important of my principles: Surround yourself with winners in your business and personal life.

"Your greatest power is the power to choose." I assure you …

If you choose to hang out with dogs you will wake up with fleas!

6

Balance your life … Give an equal measure of time and attention to …

• Family • Fitness • Spiritual Life

"The race in life is not always to the swift but to those who keep on running"

–a balanced life will keep you running.

James J. Maguire

"It's a universal law– the more we sow, the more we reap"

James J. Maguire
Founder, Philadelphia Insurance Companies

Chapter 6
On the Way to Chevway

▶ Home in Blue Bell

Frannie and Jim, Jamie, Susie, Chris, Tim, and our beautiful Megan, born on February 16, 1968

Early in 1968, when Eustace came back from Chicago excited about a new national leasing opportunity and asked me to join him on a second trip to explore a deal that, in his words, could make us "more successful than we had ever dreamed of," I refused. I wanted to be home for Frannie, eight months pregnant with our sixth child, Megan. The farthest I wanted to travel in those days was to the grass courts of the Germantown Cricket Club, where I occasionally played tennis.

I wasn't really interested in taking on a new business venture, even with a dear and greatly respected friend like Eustace. I was bringing home above-average money, had a couple of cars and a liberal expense account, all while growing my business. I was on track to double the size of the agency over the next three to four years. Life was good. Why get distracted?

But there was no escaping Eustace's persistence. He simply could not contain his enthusiasm for the Chicago deal. He implored me to meet his new partners and evaluate the insurance plan for his recently acquired car-leasing program – and that was that.

One night he called me from his mother's house, recalling both his dad and mine, dying at very young ages. "It is our responsibility to honor their lives by excelling in ours," he told me. Wow! Those words struck a vital chord with me. It was my father who made me believe in myself. Eustace was right; it was what my father would have wanted me to do.

"It is our responsibility to honor their lives by excelling in ours."

I was growing increasingly concerned about the restrictions that insurance companies were imposing on Philadelphia-area agents, so, despite my initial misgivings, I concluded that I should at least take a look and agreed to fly to Chicago with Eustace.

▶ **Four Principals of Chevway/Genway**
From left: Walter Heingartner, Eustace Wolfington, Shellman Morse, Vince Wolfington.

It was a very cold day in late February 1968 when I met the other three Chevway Corporation partners at the company's office in the Union Carbide Building on South Michigan Avenue: Vince Wolfington (Eustace's brother), Shellman Morse, and Walter Heingartner. Vince and

Shell were young bankers in training at Chase Manhattan Bank, and Walter was a New York Chevrolet dealer. Together with Eustace, they would come to be called "the four horsemen."

A month earlier, after several months of what Eustace described as "the most harrowing and difficult financial machinations" he'd ever experienced, Lehman Brothers had financed for Eustace and his partners the purchase of 1,204,000 Chevway shares, or 55 percent of the outstanding stock and controlling interest in Chevway.

Formed in 1965 and licensed by General Motors to call itself Chevway, the company franchised Chevrolet dealers to use the Chevway system for local car-rental and leasing activities. Its services included insurance, financing, marketing, billing and collection, sales training, off-lease disposal, residual valuation, and uniform national advertising.

I spent a few hours examining Chevway's existing insurance program, which was underwritten by Aetna Insurance Company through the Chicago office of Johnson & Higgins, a large national brokerage firm. I concluded two things: First, the insurance contracts were not written as I would recommend, and second, Eustace was right: this was indeed the business opportunity of a lifetime.

GM itself marketed Chevway. Chevrolet dealers wanting to enter the growing leasing and rental market were directed to Chevway by the giant automaker. In its first year of operation, Chevway processed over 8,000 vehicles for its member dealers.

Eustace first heard of Chevway, a public company, in 1967, when its then-president, Jim Van Drusen, came to Philadelphia to convince Eustace to become a member dealer. At the time, Van Drusen offhandedly mentioned that Eustace could probably gain control of Chevway for a couple of million dollars or less.

The company was being managed part-time by a group of Chevrolet dealers who provided little oversight and less vision. As a result, Chevway had racked up a huge deficit and its stock was nearly worthless. Furthermore, its accounting system was in such shambles that many disgruntled dealers had stopped making payments, thus tying up money Chevway was obligated to pay its financing partner, General Motors Acceptance Corporation (GMAC).

When Eustace and his partners took over in January 1968, Chevway was some $25 million in arrears to GMAC and had substantial operating losses. Nevertheless, the group saw potential. Eustace was convinced that car leasing to individual drivers was about to take off in the United States — in the previous six years, the estimated ratio of leased cars to all automobiles had nearly doubled, to more than 11 percent. Within 10 years, the leasing companies were expected to account for one in four cars sold in the United States.

As Vince Wolfington explained, in a traditional sale "there was no hook to bring the customer back," forcing dealers and manufacturers to spend millions of dollars to bring customers into the showroom each year. However, a lease customer had to come back into the showroom to return the car, automatically giving the dealer another sales opportunity.

In addition, while conducting their Chevway due diligence, Eustace and his partners realized the enormous value afforded by Chevway's exclusive licensing agreement with GM, the only such license GM had ever granted. Since GM had no lease program of its own, its endorsement put Chevway in a unique position to capture a large portion of GM's leasing business. The Chevway franchises, located in 27 cities, could saturate the market.

Even though Chevway was in terrible administrative and financial shape, its overall concept was sound.

Eustace was confident of his partners' ability to make the deal work administratively. Having already gained control using mostly borrowed money, they planned to turn Chevway around by standardizing advertising, rates, forms, residual values, insurance, financing, and dealership training on a national basis. Vince and Shell would put their financing experience to work on delinquent-account collection and the automation of various internal controls, while Walter would focus on developing an ongoing relationship with GMAC. It was Eustace's job to use his sales and marketing savvy to win back the confidence and loyalty of the Chevway dealers.

Even though Chevway was in terrible administrative and financial shape, its overall concept was sound.

The one thing the group still needed was precisely what I could provide, experience in underwriting automobile insurance for leasing companies. Chevway's program with Johnson & Higgins was a one-size-fits-all policy geared more toward fleets than individual drivers. I knew that other insurance companies would be vying for the account, too, which made me both nervous and energized because I would be competing with the industry big boys – Johnson & Higgins, Marsh McLennan, Alexander & Alexander, Frank B. Hall, and others.

Frannie and I had concluded that this might be a one-time opportunity to break onto the national stage. Accordingly, we carefully considered all the pros and cons. Just structuring a national program would be challenging, time consuming, and risky in that the big brokers could easily outspend me, and they had clout with the insurance companies. I also worried that working on the Chevway account could be financially costly and might hurt my Philadelphia business.

My mind and spirits were lifted when the newest addition to our family, beautiful Megan, arrived on February 16. Susie, who was almost seven when Megan was born, immediately took charge of feeding and caring for her sister, creating a lifelong bond. If I decided to pursue the Chevway account, Frannie would be left at home with five children, two of them toddlers and one an infant — while I commuted between Chicago and the insurance companies working on the account.

Despite the negatives, Frannie could see how excited I was by the opportunity. If I succeeded, I'd receive substantial commission income of course, but more than that she knew I craved the challenge: this was my first chance to compete for a national account. I instinctively knew that other insurance products could be piggybacked onto Chevway, but I put all that out of my mind until the master account was in place. Eustace had won me over.

Landing the account and setting up an operating system would take six to eight months of travel, I thought. Frannie assured me that she could manage on her own and that everything in Blue Bell would be fine. Had we known that six to eight months would stretch to six years, I doubt that either of us would have been as certain of our ability to cope as we were at the moment of decision.

I submitted proposals and met with INA and Hartford to gauge their interest. Both wanted to work with me on the Chevway deal, but after a series of meetings, I chose Hartford. The Ohio Casualty debacle, out of which Hartford had bailed me, had assured me of the company's expertise, and their enthusiasm for the Chevway opportunity was obvious. They recognized that this could be a major account. A real spirit of cooperation infused the weeks of daylong meetings and the back-and-forth negotiating that preceded the eventual proposal.

Hartford's actuaries, underwriters, and information-technology managers, led by account coordinator Al Nork, were charged with establishing the leased-auto insurance rates for every metropolitan area across the country. First, though, Chevway had to tell me where its existing leased vehicles were located and project where the next 8,000 were likely to be located. If all of the new leases were in New York City, for example, the composite insurance rate would be considerably higher than if the leases were in Tulsa, Oklahoma.

Initially, Hartford wanted to provide the collision and comprehensive coverage, too. But I chose to place that segment of the program with Motors Insurance Company (MIC), a General Motors subsidiary, for two reasons: to create a new underwriter relationship, and to improve our access to GM dealerships.

With a proposal in hand, Eustace and I headed to Chicago. Neither of us had traveled much beyond Philadelphia except when we were in the service or on vacation. Now here we were in the fabled "city of broad shoulders," America's third-largest metropolis, with me preparing to make my first pitch for a national account in Chevway's boardroom. I was a little nervous but confident and positive, knowing I was well prepared.

"If Jim was nervous," Eustace says, "he didn't show it. And though the decision wasn't reached immediately, I knew before Jim even finished that he had won the account, hands down."

The look on the board members' faces told me they were impressed by my presentation. But it wasn't until later that evening, over dinner with Eustace and Shell, that I learned I had won the account.

The next morning, I called Al Nork to set up a meeting at Hartford's headquarters in Connecticut. Lots of pieces still had to be knitted together before we could proceed. Over the next three months, Al and his people flew in and out of Chicago more often than any of us care to remember.

"If Jim was nervous," Eustace says, "he didn't show it."

I rented a hotel room on the 12th floor of the Sheraton Chicago, directly across the street from the new Chevway headquarters at 500 North Michigan Avenue. During the summer of 1968, after everyone had gone home, I spent countless hours working on various models and penetration schedules for the Chevway marketing plan. Many nights, I walked up the 12 flights to my room just to get some needed exercise (this was in the days before hotel gyms). I usually called Frannie about 9 P.M., after the kids were in bed. It was an exciting time in business for me but a lonely and difficult time for Frannie, though she rarely complained.

I flew home from O'Hare every Friday at 6 P.M., spent all day Saturday and Sunday morning with Frannie and the kids, and then returned to Chicago on a 2 P.M. Sunday flight. The only break in this routine came when I traveled to Hartford. It was grueling but I loved it, though my infamously short temper did at times show the strain.

One Monday, Ken Wilcutts and I were scheduled to fly up to Connecticut on a 7:30 A.M. Allegheny Airlines flight out of Philadelphia. Allegheny, which had open seating, was notorious for overbooking, so I arrived at the gate early and was first in line to board when word of a flight delay came over the loudspeaker.

Thinking I could grab a cup of coffee, I left my spot in line. While I was away, the delay was reversed and the Allegheny agent started the boarding process. Now I was at the end of the line and three-quarters of the passengers had already boarded. With only three of us left to board, the agent announced that the plane was full. The next flight didn't depart until 11:15 A.M., too late for me to keep my lunch date with Al Nork's boss.

I had arrived early just so I could prevent something like this from happening, only to be caught up in an airline departure snafu that was now costing me my seat. Out of sheer frustration, I started raising hell and pushing toward the door, preventing the agent from closing it. When he grabbed my arm, that was all it took for me to explode and let him have it with my briefcase.

Security guards and the police converged on the scene almost immediately, and I was hauled off to the security office, with Wilcutts following at a safe distance, trying to act as if he didn't know me. After checking to see if I had a police record or any unpaid traffic fines, I was released.

Such embarrassments aside, the challenge of building a national presence and the business successes and pleasures of those years went a long way toward negating the negatives. For one thing, I would have missed the good fortune of working with Al Nork had I not embarked on this journey.

Al knew how to get things done in a big company. Once assigned to manage the Chevway account, he handled every detail, initially getting the actuaries to focus on understanding the risks associated with the original 8,000-car account and then prodding them to do the same for the projected first-year addition of 8,000 vehicles to the fleet. And when I suggested writing a $50,000 self-insured retention, something not done before, he was a strong advocate and provided me with the actuarial information I needed to keep Chevway from overloading the program in ways that would drain its self-funded account.

The IT department helped me to devise a computerized system to monitor the insured vehicles and issue insurance certificates in dealerships across the country. By tracking claim coverage, I could make sure the fleet average was at or below the composite rate, in turn preventing an inadequate rate from developing.

September 1, 1968, was designated as the policy start date, and by late August, all the required paperwork, systems, and claims apparatus were in place. Now I was ready to take Eustace and his partners to Connecticut to meet the Hartford operating team and Harry Williams, the company's president.

I'll never forget the day we arrived at the home office. There in the lobby rotunda, on a big board balanced on an easel, was a sign proclaiming in large letters, "Welcome, Jim Maguire and Chevway." What a kick that was! In later years, I copied the "welcome" sign idea to greet visitors to our offices.

I was living proof that hard work, coupled with a belief in one's own abilities, could make dreams come true.

Harry Williams was very gracious and knowledgeable about the Chevway program. During lunch in the executive dining room, he congratulated our group on its partnership with General Motors. As we were leaving, he shook my hand and in front of the assemblage thanked me for "favoring Hartford with this national account."

The VIP treatment I received that day flooded me with a tremendous feeling of accomplishment. I was living proof that hard work, coupled with a belief in one's own abilities, could make dreams come true. It was as if my father was with me that day telling me to believe in myself.

▶ 1969 - There were only five
Susie, Chris, Jim, Frannie, Megan, Jamie, Tim

I traveled the country installing the Chevway/Genway account, while Frannie managed the homefront.

*"Dream big–
dreams do come true"*

James J. Maguire
Founder, Philadelphia Insurance Companies

Chapter 7

Shifting into High Gear

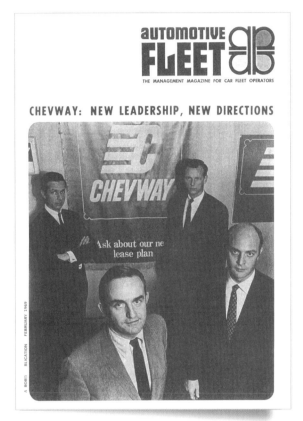

> ▶ Four Principals of Chevway/Genway

Clockwise from left: Eustace Wolfington, Vince Wolfington, Shellman Morse, Walter Heingartner.

I took Eustace and his partners a year of intense, 12-hour workdays to turn Chevway around. By year-end 1969, they had erased a pre-acquisition operating loss of $262,704, putting the company securely in the black, with operating income of $842,000. Chevway's success earned recognition in the February 1969 edition of *Automotive Fleet* magazine, which featured the "Four Horsemen" on the front cover. The article, entitled "Chevway: New Leadership, New Directions," was a splendid introduction for the revamped Chevway. It gave the new management a national stage to explain the company's previous problems, their solutions, and the hard-earned success that followed.

I was especially pleased when Eustace said that Chevway's insurance plan was "the most important part" of the package. Here was the national recognition I had hoped for when I had contemplated Eustace's offer. The positive publicity would mark the Maguire Insurance Agency as a leader in the leasing and rental industry.

Almost overnight, my agency went from a 12-man operation selling insurance in Philadelphia to a national company with access to every Chevrolet dealer in the United States. Operationally, though, I had to make sure the Philadelphia office would run smoothly without my day-to-day guidance. I had people I trusted: I promoted Ken Wilcutts to vice president and chief operating officer and Arlette Chellis, already chief financial officer, to office manager. Ruth and six administrative assistants rounded out our Philadelphia staff.

▶ 1969 - Lake Point Tower
I rented an apartment on the 70th floor and was one of the first tenants. My office at 500 N. Michigan Ave. was within walking distance.

It was a heady time for all concerned.

My work with Chevway kept me in Chicago most of the time, and I was getting tired of hotel living. In mid-1969, I signed a two-year lease on a spacious, two-bedroom apartment on the 70th floor of the new Lake Point Tower. The complex was a beautiful, clover-leaf-shaped building with spectacular views of Lake Michigan, not far from Chevway headquarters. Frannie flew out to help me furnish and decorate the apartment. She spent several days shopping at Marshall Field's under the tutelage of a store decorator, gathering everything one might need for comfortable apartment living – from furniture to dishes and silver to soap and cooking utensils (the latter never used).

The Struggle for Independence

By the spring of 1969, the insurance division of Chevway had become an important profit center and a key marketing tool for the company. I was an integral part of the management team, but I still operated as an independent contractor. Shell Morse began a campaign to make the Maguire Agency part of the Chevway holding company, so that the two entities' income could be consolidated.

Shell talked about the advantages of owning stock in a public company, being a partner on the management team, and sitting on the board. I said, "Thanks but no thanks." I owned my company, and that's how I wanted it to stay. I argued that Chevway got more value from my remaining independent.

Shell flatly disagreed, so I finally revealed my personal reason for staying independent: "Someday I wanted to bring my kids into the agency." Still, Shell persisted and I resisted throughout several meetings – until he delivered an ultimatum: Sell 80 percent of the agency to Tetra, or Chevway would be forced to find a new broker.

I asked Eustace to get Shell to back off. Instead, to my dismay, Eustace gave me another sales pitch, though softer in tone and without an ultimatum. "We're a public company," he said, "and we have to do what's best for our stockholders." With no one taking my side, it was a fait accompli. I was unhappy but felt I had no choice but to give in to Shell's hardball tactics, rationalizing that giving up my independence to hold onto my first national account was the inevitable cost of success.

The proposal Shell laid out valued the agency at a flattering $1 million, 80 percent of which translated to 31,312 shares at $25.55 per share the day we settled. Shortly thereafter I was elected to the Board of Directors and received 10,000 additional shares.

Dream House Discovered

With the sale of the agency completed and Frannie carrying our seventh child, we began looking for a larger house in or near Chestnut Hill, a suburb of Philadelphia and home to Norwood Academy, the private Catholic school that Jamie and Susie attended. The day Frannie and I first saw the house on Flourtown Avenue with our realtor, Stan Smullen, we fell in love – even though we were only allowed to see the ground floor of the main house. The second and third floors were "not made up," we were told.

The house was on an estate built in 1911 by Francis J. Gowen, a member of a prominent family long a major presence in Pennsylvania business and society. The estate was purchased in 1916 by the Lavino family, which accounts for the inscription clearly visible at the property's entrance. "ONIVAL," the family name reversed, is deeply inscribed on the imposing eight-foot pillars flanking the iron gates. Ted Lavino, Jr., son of the chairman of the Lavino Shipping Company, an important business in Philadelphia, and the current occupant of the house, had quietly put it on the market.

The five-acre property featured formal gardens and brick patios. There was a perfectly manicured lawn off the front patio that I immediately saw as a football field for the children. Every new feature we saw – the greenhouse with attached cottage, the four-bedroom apartment over the garage, the kidney-shaped pool fenced with wrought iron – prompted approving looks between me and Frannie. This was the house we were looking for.

As we stepped onto the front porch after our truncated tour, I asked Smullen, "What's the asking price?" And Stan, with the junior Lavino standing beside him, said, "It's still $150,000, right, Ted?" Ted nodded yes. I pulled out my checkbook and wrote a check for $15,000. I handed it to Stan and said, "Let's go back to your office and draft an agreement of sale." An hour later, junior and I signed the agreement, and Frannie and I thought we had just bought our dream house.

▶ **August 1, 1969 - The Maguire homestead**
Senior Lavino offered to pay me $50,000 to
cancel the sale.

Not so fast. It turned out that Ted Lavino, Sr. hadn't been consulted and wasn't interested in selling the family estate. Though the house had been a wedding gift to his son and his wife, Linda, the senior Lavino claimed that his son was not authorized to sell the property. He relayed this news to Stan Mullen on Monday morning, two days after we signed the agreement.

The senior Lavino, lamenting that the home had been in the family for over 50 years, said Ted Jr. had made a major mistake. Stan told him to take the matter up with Mr. Maguire's attorney, John McCreesh. Later that day, he called John and offered to pay me $50,000 to cancel the contract. I turned down the offer without a moment's hesitation. I had already called my friend Bill Volmer at Philadelphia National Bank and arranged a margin loan against my Chevway stock to fund the purchase.

We moved into our new home on August 1, 1969. Frannie gave birth to Colleen exactly one week later, on August 8. No matter how many kids followed Colleen, we knew we'd never be cramped for space. Every piece of furniture we brought with us from the four-bedroom Blue Bell house fit into two rooms with no crowding.

I stayed in Philadelphia for a few weeks after Colleen's birth. With six kids – now evenly divided between boys and girls – I gained a considerable understanding of what Frannie had gone through in my absence. So later that year, as Eustace and I were finishing a presentation to Bay Area GM dealers at the Fairmont Hotel in San Francisco, we called Frannie and Eustace's wife, Marcy, and asked them to meet us the following day en route to a week in Hawaii.

▸ August 8, 1969 - Colleen Maguire
Colleen arrived one week after moving into our new home.

Most wives probably would have hung up on us after telling us we were nuts to even think they could arrange for babysitters and such on the spur of the moment. But Frannie and Marcy were game. They called back a few hours later to say they were on their way. On Friday at noon, Frannie and Marcy stepped off one plane in San Francisco and together we boarded another to Hawaii.

That vacation was one of the best we ever had. It was just the unexpected respite Frannie and I needed. The second night at dinner, Marcy and I ordered mahi-mahi and got food poisoning, which kept us both down for 24 hours. But we recovered and went on with the vacation.

▸ November 1969 - Don Ho Restaurant
Eustace and Marcy Wolfington with Jim and Frannie in Hawaii at the Don Ho Restaurant.
"Meet us in San Francisco on Friday morning and we'll take you to Hawaii."

"Our greatest power is the power to choose"

James J. Maguire

Founder, Philadelphia Insurance Companies

Chapter 8
Looking to the Future

▶ January 20, 1970 - WHEELWAYS brochure
"Ahead of the Curve"

Even as I settled into our new home and my new role as a Chevway shareholder, I hadn't forgotten the invaluable lesson I learned when competitors flocked to copy my early success in the deaf community: When you find a successful niche market, you have to be prepared for the day you may lose it, because niche markets typically have a limited life. So prepare I did.

The success of Chevway's insurance program and my contact with Chevway licensees started me thinking about a complete and comprehensive insurance package for dealerships. I took a page out of my earlier experience in auditing potential clients, and started quietly surveying them about their insurance requirements. At the time, dealership coverage was expensive, fragmented, and lacked a focused national program or marketing effort. I was already working with more than half the Chevrolet dealers in the country, providing coverage for their leasing and rentals. I was endorsed by GM and Motors Insurance Company (MIC). The exposure and credibility afforded me by the Chevway account made it a perfect time to market a companion product.

When you find a successful niche market, you have to be prepared for the day you may lose it.

Automobile dealers were buying five or six different policies to insure their business. From talking to them I learned what they really wanted was a comprehensive package policy. So I developed an all-risk policy for buildings and contents, which included business interruption; garage liability; floor-plan physical damage; advertisers' liability; criminal acts; destruction of valuable papers and records; damage to neon signs, plate glass, boilers, and machinery; and workers' compensation. It was comprehensive and the first package policy for dealers, plus premiums were based on the dealers' gross receipts ... another first!

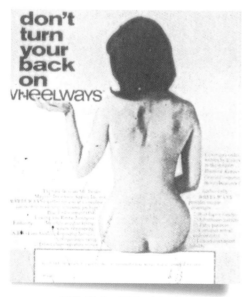

▶ 1970 - National Print Advertising
Response was off the charts.

I christened my new product the WHEELWAYS Automobile Dealers Package Plan of Insurance. Because of my tight relationship with Hartford and Motors Insurance, both companies agreed almost instantly to underwrite my new product. WHEELWAYS was a top-quality product for the auto dealer and a phenomenal deal for my agency. Hartford's mass-marketing department, headed up by Jim Brennan, agreed to introduce it to the company's U.S. offices with instructions to channel all account applications to my Philadelphia staff for processing. We would do the preliminary underwriting and then send the accounts to Hartford's Philadelphia office for final pricing. Ken Wilcutts and Joe Werner became my underwriting experts, and were the point men as new accounts started pouring in.

On January 20, 1970, the Hartford marketing department sent a two-page memo to all of its officers and departmental and regional managers announcing the program. It said: "We are most anxious to have WHEELWAYS succeed and request your wholehearted cooperation in referring interested agencies to the Maguire Agency." Attached to the memo was the four-color WHEELWAYS brochure.

HARTFORD FIRE INSURANCE COMPANY
HARTFORD ACCIDENT AND INDEMNITY COMPANY
HARTFORD LIFE INSURANCE COMPANY

CITIZENS INSURANCE COMPANY OF NEW JERSEY
NEW YORK UNDERWRITERS INSURANCE COMPANY
TWIN CITY FIRE INSURANCE COMPANY

THE HARTFORD INSURANCE GROUP
HARTFORD PLAZA, HARTFORD, CONNECTICUT 06115

January 20, 1970

TO DEPARTMENTAL AND REGIONAL MANAGERS
    Attention: Agency Superintendents
    (Copies to Officers, Assistant Managers, Office Managers and
    Office Administration Superintendents)

            Marketing Department Administrative Bulletin #84
            "WHEELWAYS" Automobile Dealers Insurance Program

"WHEELWAYS" -a program of financial services (including: appraisal service, automated billing, broad insurance coverage and premium financing among others) designed expressly for the franchised automobile dealer-was introduced at the National Automobile Dealers Association convention in Miami this week by the Maguire Insurance Agency of Pennsylvania, Inc.

"WHEELWAYS" was developed by and is a registered service mark of the Maguire Agency; however, it will be marketed exclusively through licensed local insurance producers under a special brokers contract with the Maguire Agency.

Although "WHEELWAYS" is a Maguire Insurance Agency program, the HARTFORD INSURANCE GROUP is intensely interested in it. We worked closely with the agency in developing the insurance segment of the program; and are the underwriter for a major portion of the coverage. Our participation and support is an example of our continuing experimentation with Association/Franchise merchandising of property and casualty insurance; and is evidence of our conviction that this concept of insurance merchandising can be applied

▶ January 20, 1970 - Hartford announces WHEELWAYS

That same month, I introduced the WHEELWAYS program with a major presentation at the National Automobile Dealers Association conference in Miami. Like my earlier success in solving insurance for the deaf, I considered this to be another high point in my career. Over a three-day period, we collected business cards and invitations to contact dealers from all over the United States.

▶ 1970 - WHEELWAYS introduction
National Automobile Dealers Association, Miami, Florida

By 1971, the program was so successful that Hartford set up a special unit to rate, quote, and issue accounts. I hired regional salespeople and opened offices in Chicago, New York, Fort Lauderdale, San Francisco, and Atlanta to help the Hartford branches and their agents understand the nuances of the program, market it, and sign up accounts. The Hartford offices across the country initiated an all-out plan to introduce our program to their agents.

Managing and overseeing these two huge accounts took a lot of energy. When I wasn't meeting with the Four Horsemen in Chevway's New York office, I was working with the Chevway sales representatives in Chicago or at one of the company's regional offices. I also had to attend meetings with actuaries and underwriters from Motors Insurance or the Hartford and work in the field with my WHEELWAYS marketing team.

Revving General Motors

A few months earlier, General Motors, under the leadership of its president, Ed Cole, had announced that Chevway would be renamed Genway Corporation and would be exclusively licensed to market its services to all GM dealers. That coup traced back to 1969, when Chevway bid unsuccessfully to purchase National Car Rental.

In the late '60s, Budget Car Rental used mostly Chrysler products, Hertz rented Fords, and GM was angling to work a deal with National. So in the spring of 1969, when GM's fleet and leasing division alerted Chevway that Jimmie Ling, the CEO of Ling-Tempco-Vought, was looking to sell his stake in National, Vince, Eustace, and I were invited to Detroit to discuss the acquisition with Ed Cole.

Cole was very interested in the Chevway concept and a strong supporter of its new management. He made it clear that he wanted Chevway to acquire National Car Rental so they could rent GM products. To facilitate the acquisition, Cole arranged a $35 million loan through Chase Manhattan Bank for Genway ... the amount needed to buy Jimmy Ling's interest. Unfortunately, Chevway lost out to Household Finance in a bidding war after Cole had secured the loan.

The bright side of this embarrassing debacle was that Vince and Eustace cemented their already strong relationship with Cole and, by extension, GM. He pledged to support them after the failed bid, and later that year made good on his promise by giving the newly renamed Genway

THE CHASE MANHATTAN BANK   L 34641
National Association
New York, N.Y.

Date   May 2, 1969   1-2
                                                        210
Pay   CHASE MANHATTAN BANK $160229GT AND 50 CTS

to the order of

Ling Temco Vought, Inc.

AUTHORIZED SIGNATURE

THE CHASE MANHATTAN BANK   L 34642
National Association
New York, N.Y.

Date   MAY 2, 1969   1-2
                                                        210
Pay   THIRTY-THREE MILLION FIVE HUNDRED SIXTY-SIX THOUSAND $ 33,566,400.00
            FOUR HUNDRED AND 00/100 DOLLARS

to the order of

LING-TEMCO-VOUGHT, INC. --

AUTHORIZED SIGNATURE

▸ **May 1969 - Bid to purchase National Car Rental**
Ed Cole, president of General Motors, arranged a $35 million loan from Chase Manhattan Bank for
Chevway to purchase National Car Rental.

the exclusive marketing rights to all GM dealers, plus, he promised financial incentives for enrolling new dealers and growing the fleet. We were understandably excited by Cole's show of support.

When the agreement was announced in the third quarter of 1969, Genway employees, management, and dealers, along with knowledgeable GM personnel, started to buy Genway stock. Consequently, the price rocketed to $38 dollars a share, leaving me feeling that Genway stock wasn't such a bad idea after all. In the spring of 1970, Genway officially began marketing its services to all General Motors dealers.

As summer rolled around, I alternated between exhilaration and exhaustion. Both the Genway and WHEELWAYS programs were extraordinarily successful, and I was constantly on the road. During the week, I traveled to wherever Genway was being introduced, then I'd hop a Friday flight to Bermuda to spend the weekend with my family in the home Frannie had rented.

Though I had little time to savor my accomplishments, the contacts and reputation I had built with General Motors – not to mention the reflected glow from Genway – were propelling me to ever-higher highs. A GM fleet executive, trying to sell Budget Rent a Car on switching to GM products, arranged for me to meet Budget's president, Morris Belzberg, to discuss fleet insurance. I immediately connected with the outgoing and dynamic Belzberg, and almost overnight, I secured the Budget airport-rental account across the United States.

▶ June 1970 - Another major national account

Budget locations that were corporately owned were automatically enrolled in the program. But the company's licensees, comprising about 40 percent of the Budget locations nationwide, were free to make an independent buying decision. So with the licensees in mind, I prepared carefully for my presentation to Budget's annual convention in Montreal. When half of the licensees joined the program within the first year, I was pleased – and more aware than ever of the potential this new niche represented. Our sales representatives, who initially called on only the Budget airport accounts, started calling on all the car-rental agencies. We quickly generated a base of over 7,000 new customers.

Over the course of that summer, Genway put together a presentation and GM's Fleet Leasing division scheduled meetings aimed at introducing us to every General Motors dealer across the country. Eustace and the Genway sales team hired field representatives, opened additional field offices, and launched a national advertising campaign. I went on the road with the Genway marketing team.

The reception was exciting. Dealers signed up in unprecedented numbers. At one of the biggest meetings in San Francisco, every GM dealer in the region was required to attend. After an elaborate lunch, I was introduced by the GM district manager as the national expert in leasing insurance. Just try to keep that accolade from going to your head.

For the most part, however, I continued to operate as I always had. At the end of my workday, I put in my regular hour of exercise. No weekday was complete until I'd called Frannie and had an update on the goings-on of the children, after which I prepared for my next meeting. On the weekends, I'd fly to wherever my family was, be it Bermuda or Philadelphia. And no matter where we were, Sunday morning would find the family at Mass.

The Maguire Insurance Agency had witnessed extraordinary changes over a span of just three years. No one outside the Philadelphia area had ever heard of us in 1968. But by the end of 1970, the chances were good that anyone who leased or rented a car anywhere in the United States was insured through our agency.

Unbeknownst to me, trouble lay just ahead.

By the end of 1970 if you leased or rented a car in the U.S. it was probably insured through our agency.

*"Overcoming problems
is the key
to achievement"*

James J. Maguire
Founder, Philadelphia Insurance Companies

Chapter 9
Speed Bumps

▸ **1970 summer vacation after an extended trip across the United States** marketing
the Genway GM leasing program to dealers.
(left to right) Jim, Frannie, Megan, Tim, Joe Sweeney, Susie, Jamie, Chris *(standing)*,
(in back) Cecil Sweeney

Summer was fast receding in late August 1970 and I was exhausted from non-stop traveling when Frannie and I packed up the children for a much-needed vacation at my sister Joan's cabin in Brandon, Vermont. It was around noon when we pulled into the Sweeney retreat on Lake Dunmore. Nestled in the heart of the Champlain Valley near the Green Mountains, the cabin had been the site of many happy hours spent with Joan, her husband, Alan, and their family in summers past.

Relaxation was not part of our vacation vocabulary. Between the Maguires and the Sweeneys, 10 kids were stuffed into that cabin, ranging in age from our one-year-old Colleen to their 14-year-old Sean. Keeping everyone occupied and out of harm's way took some doing.

Those carefree, activity-filled summer days at the lake took me back to the best parts of my own childhood at Crystal Lake. To this day, no Maguire get-together is complete without some kind of ball flying through the air or kids romping across the lawn to beat a cousin to the finish line.

Early on the fourth day of our stay, though, I got an urgent phone call from my banker, Bill Volmer. Genway was in trouble. The share price had dropped below a dollar – down from a high of $38 – and the NASDAQ had suspended trading. Bill was well-versed in Genway's business and had been involved when I decided to margin my Genway stock in lieu of taking a mortgage on our Flourtown Avenue home. But now, the disintegrating value of the stock meant my $1,500,000 holding in Genway stock was gone and I had to meet a $150,000 margin call to cover the loan.

I asked Bill if he wanted me to return to Philadelphia. "Don't worry," he said. "You can see me next week when you get back from vacation." (Upon my return, I settled the margin call by securing a traditional $150,000 mortgage on our home.)

"There were children everywhere, and Uncle Jim was like the scoutmaster." – Sean Sweeney

Within minutes of Bill's call, Bernie Steibel, one of Genway's corporate lawyers, phoned with identical news, but he was able to shed more light on the situation. According to Bernie, the stock crashed after someone leaked information that the GMAC audit division had turned up evidence that Genway was "out of trust." In other words, there was supposedly a significant shortfall in the dollars collected by Genway that were owed to GMAC.

Here's what had happened: When Ed Cole awarded Chevway-cum-Genway the exclusive license to market its leasing and rental franchise to all GM dealers, the Four Horsemen began rolling out the new program before the subsidy contract was finalized. As the contract negotiations dragged on and costs of the rollout mounted, lease payments that were supposed to go to GMAC were being used to fill the holes in Genway's budget. We were all operating in good faith: no one seemed overly concerned with getting the contract completed.

Eustace and his partners planned to resolve the shortfall once the contract was signed and the promised GM dollars (which were accumulating) started flowing to Genway. (Cole had proposed paying Genway a fixed amount for each GM dealer signed into the program and an additional override on each vehicle leased.) If need be, Eustace had assurances of a bridge loan from Jack Wilson at First Pennsylvania Bank. Even though things looked bleak on that August day, I still believed we would resolve the problem once we met with Ed Cole.

Frannie immediately offered to help relieve any financial pressure by tightening our household budget. She asked if she should cancel the Bermuda rental for the following summer and get our deposit back. "Absolutely not!" I roared. "Nobody needs to know what's going on – besides, this whole matter is simply based on a lack of communication." Having gone through all those years when Ruth strode through the house turning off lights and lowering the heat, I didn't want my children to worry about our financial situation.

The Genway Story: Short but Spectacular

Genway was on a roll and spirits were high when GM announced the new contract.

The relationship with GM's president, the extra attention from the fleet division, plus the whirlwind success they were realizing were all intoxicating. I believe, however, that management was a bit naïve in the ways of business.

The audit shortfall obviously wasn't good, but the real problem, as it turned out (unbeknownst to Genway), was an earlier power play within GM which proved to be the coup de grace for Genway.

In May of 1970, the legendary president of the United Auto Workers (UAW), Walter Reuther, had been killed in a plane crash. Perhaps trying to prove his mettle, Leonard Woodcock, Reuther's successor, decided to instigate the first strike against General Motors since 1946.

▶ **May 1970 · Leonard Woodcock**
Walter Reuther, legendary president of the United Auto Workers (UAW), was killed in a private plane crash. His successor was Leonard Woodcock.

Without warning, the UAW members walked off their jobs on September 14 of that year, halting GM assembly lines and opening the way for the financial arm of GM – less friendly toward Genway – to seize control of strike negotiations.

Most analysts predicted a quick settlement, theorizing that Woodcock did not have Reuther's reputation or clout. They were wrong. The strike dragged on, leaving GM dealers across the country without cars and Genway with substantial new overhead costs, nothing to lease, and still no funding support from GM for its dealer program.

Lulled by Ed Cole's friendly relations with Vince and Eustace, Shell and the other Genway principals, including me, didn't suspect that behind the scenes GMAC was preparing to compete with Genway. Indeed, when GMAC first announced its leasing program, it was widely viewed as just another financing plan, without insurance and with none of Genway's services. By the time we saw what was happening, Cole had been pushed aside, and GMAC's CEO, John O. Zimmerman – commonly referred to as J.O.Z. and very aloof in demeanor – was calling all the shots.

Less than a year earlier, Cole had made a single phone call to Chase Manhattan Bank to arrange an unsecured $35 million loan for Genway to purchase National Car Rental. Now, not only was Genway's GM funding agreement stalled (presumably by J.O.Z.), Zimmerman also summarily dismissed any efforts to solve the out-of-trust delinquency with a bridge loan, a possible sale of stock on Wall Street, or an advance from GM. Some nasty words flew between J.O.Z. and Shell Morse. I suspect this animosity also played a part in J.O.Z.'s decision to play hardball with Genway. In any event, it was clear that GMAC wanted no competition from Genway.

▶ **The strike**
Shortly after becoming president of the UAW in 1970, Leonard Woodcock led union members in a historic 67-day strike against General Motors.

I was with Eustace in GMAC's 52nd-floor executive suite in New York, overlooking Central Park, on that mid-November day in 1970 when J.O.Z. ran Genway and the Four Horsemen off the road. J.O.Z.'s attorney strongly suggested that they sign a "walk-away" consent agreement and surrender Genway to GMAC, thereby canceling their personal liabilities for being $25 million out of trust. I was against signing any such agreement, asking the obvious question: "Where's Ed Cole and what about the funding agreement?"

I pulled Eustace aside and said, "Let's just leave. You don't have to sign anything today, and you need to get a lawyer."

The meeting was adjourned until the following afternoon, giving me time to contact my attorney, John McCreesh, who immediately drove up from Philadelphia. He told me not to sign anything. Meanwhile, Eustace learned from Jack Wilson that J.O.Z. had blocked the bridge loan by suggesting that there were "unanswered accounting questions."

The next day, the Four Horsemen, none of whom had engaged personal counsel, caved in to GMAC's hardball and signed the walk-away agreement. They felt they had no other viable options.

Eustace was distraught for the next six months and couldn't talk about Genway without sinking into depression. He felt responsible for the loss of Genway, shouldering the blame for allowing GMAC to steal his idea and for not fighting back when they pushed him and his partners out.

I wasn't depressed, just worried. Although I refused to sign anything, an 80 percent stake in Maguire Insurance was now owned by GMAC. What should I do?

Nothing, John McCreesh advised. "Let's face it, you're an afterthought," he rightly pointed out. The best thing for me to do was to just sit tight. Although we had the Genway account, the Maguire Agency had a significantly reduced value without me. I could always go back to Philadelphia with WHEELWAYS and start anew. GMAC might have control of Genway and my agency, but I hadn't signed a non-compete and they certainly didn't own Jim Maguire, the WHEELWAYS program, or the airport rent-a-car business.

In retrospect, the out-of-trust accusation was nothing more than a smokescreen scare tactic designed by GMAC to put Genway out of business. I had no expectations about continuing to service the Genway account. However, I felt they would need my expertise at least for a while.

The week after Genway went down, I got a call from New York to meet with Frank Worthing, executive vice president of the Motors Insurance Company. He was the point man on the Genway account and we had developed a close relationship. Frank told me that GMAC was planning to systematically run off the Genway leases and substitute its own program, complete with direct billing, advertising, and insurance. He asked me to work with him in securing the liability coverage. Nothing was resolved at the meeting about ownership of my company, although Frank did tell me that GMAC wasn't interested long-term in owning my agency.

I decided, after talking to John McCreesh, to work with Worthing, so I approached the Insurance Company of North America (INA) instead of going back to Hartford. Why INA and not Hartford? INA was a Philadelphia-based company and an active underwriter in my office. Also, like any

> ▶ **1972 - After the demise of Genway**
> **Insurance package for General Motors**

good insurance man, I wanted to spread the risk. Hartford was already underwriting Genway, the WHEELWAYS program, and all of my airport-rental business. It made sense to bring a new underwriter into the mix. After a little back and forth, the liability piece for GMAC was put in place.

As we prepared for the rollout of GMAC's leasing program to GM dealers, there were a myriad of details which consumed my time and attention. Following John McCreesh's advice I said nothing about the 80 percent ownership and went to work putting the leasing program in place. Don Snell, a home-office underwriting manager, and I started making plans to fly around the country making presentations, arranged by GMAC, to their dealers.

The Rollout

Our first session – planned as a practice run – was a nightmare. We landed in Memphis, Tennessee, the night before our scheduled 9 A.M. presentation. A freak snowstorm had blown through that afternoon, followed by rising temperatures that turned the snow into lakes of slush. Shuttle buses were out of service, so after a three-block walk from the terminal to our rental car, my shoes and trouser cuffs were soggy, and both Don and I were half frozen. By the time we reached our hotel, the restaurant had closed, leaving our stomachs growling. The next morning, only a third of the expected dealers showed up for our presentation. The trip's one semi-bright spot was the opportunity it gave us to rehearse before taking our presentation to the wider national audience of GM dealers.

Shortly after Don and I returned from Memphis, Frank Worthing announced that Tom Patton, a GMAC vice president, wanted to join us for lunch at New York's Plaza Hotel. He was a young, very pleasant man with a simple and straightforward message: GMAC was not interested in owning the Maguire Agency and was prepared to sell its 80 percent stake back to me for

$250,000. I was pleased but still wary of handing over a quarter of a million dollars. What I really wanted was GMAC's assurance that I would be the insurance agent of record for its new lease program, which I now realized was going to be substantially bigger than Genway. I asked John McCreesh to accompany me to my second meeting with Patton.

John arrived wearing his trademark gray-felt Stetson hat and got right to the point, rejecting straight-line principal payments. He negotiated for me to pay whatever I could afford at intervals of my choosing, so long as I paid 6 percent interest per annum and paid off the $250,000 within seven years. Finally, and most importantly, Tom Patton willingly agreed to make me the broker of record for the GMAC lease program, at least until my debt was fully satisfied.

As I geared up to service the GMAC program, which I called "Endorsement One," the future looked bright. WHEELWAYS was enjoying a steady flow of new business from both our Hartford and non-Hartford brokers, and the airport-rental business was prospering. Introducing the GMAC leasing program, however, would keep me on the road making presentations in every major city in the United States for the next year, leaving Frannie and my young children in Philadelphia.

Travel time was the least of my worries and a sacrifice I was prepared to make. The major drawback to this assignment was that GMAC wanted me to continue servicing the Genway runoff. My relationship with Genway's new management at this point was extremely unpleasant. I tried my best to get along with them, but the two hired guns in charge of shutting down the Genway operation didn't reciprocate. CEO Derrick Draycott and CFO Bruce McDougall made it clear they didn't like me and wanted me gone. Genway's previous management, me included, were openly derided as a "bunch of crooks" who misappropriated GMAC funds. The pair made me hate the very thought of going to the Chicago office.

Though my business life was turbulent, there was great joy in the Maguire household when, on November 3, 1971, our eighth child and fourth daughter was born. We named our little tiebreaker Caroline, inspired by Neil Diamond's song, "Sweet Caroline." But halfway through the ride home from the hospital, Frannie burst into tears, sobbing, "She doesn't look like a Caroline. She's a Franny," referring to her much-loved maternal grandmother.

When we stepped into the house that gloriously sunny Saturday, we proudly introduced Franny to her brothers, sisters, aunts, uncles, and grandmothers. The following Monday, I mailed a revised application to the Pennsylvania registry of births in Harrisburg, officially changing Caroline's name to Frances Mary. Naturally, we quickly began calling her little Franny.

In early 1972, I sold the converted grocery store on West Chelten Avenue and moved to larger offices on Presidential Boulevard in Bala Cynwyd, Pennsylvania. The best way to pay off my GMAC debt, I believed, was not to cut corners or become conservative, but to continue to grow.

My strategy centered around retaining the regional offices I had opened to support the rapidly growing WHEELWAYS program, while also adding new ones to strengthen our national presence. I opened a small office in Garden City, New York, and moved the Chicago office, which was next to Genway, to Oakbrook, where rents were lower and the daily verbal abuse of Draycott and McDougall was out of earshot. Ken Wilcutts, who had been running our Philadelphia office, relocated to Chicago to manage the Midwest region from Oakbrook.

We established another new office in Dallas. Our Atlanta office, managed by Jack Abernathy, remained open and served as a base from which to market in the Southeast.

In early 1973, I purchased The Dave Carlson Agency in Boston. Dave, a smart insurance man with a classic Boston accent, had been one of the first Hartford agents to write auto-dealership insurance in the WHEELWAYS program. I also bought the Dennis Wilson Agency in Los Angeles. Dennis was another Hartford agent and early convert to the WHEELWAYS program. Roger Sarver, a former Genway representative, came aboard and opened up shop in his hometown of Detroit. And we established an exclusive agreement in Providence, Rhode Island, with the John Crowley Agency, another agent enrolled to market WHEELWAYS.

Selling is not rocket science; it's knocking on doors.

As we were expanding, Genway was in runoff mode and laying off its top salespeople, whom I was happy to hire. Already knowledgeable about my products and customers, the Genway cast-offs were able to start producing business immediately. To further support our expansion, I contracted with a group of creative young advertising professionals who worked wonders with a modest annual budget. Thanks to their creativity and the hard work of my salespeople, our business doubled over the next few years.

Despite our good fortune, I had never forgotten the basic lesson I learned early in my career: Selling is not rocket science; it's knocking on doors – the same doors over and over again if necessary. To impart that lesson to our new regional salespeople, I regularly traveled to the field offices and helped them hone their skills. I accompanied them on sales calls and oversaw their follow-up procedures. The Rule of 21 was born on those regional jaunts: I told our new representatives to never remove a potential customer's name from their files until they had called on the prospect for at least 21 years.

The Rule of 21 was born on those regional jaunts.

The hard work we put in to making our leasing and rental program a success was furthered by a national trend: independent leasing companies were springing up all across the country. Given that we offered insurance protection for both the lessee/driver and the leasing company, we were well positioned to take advantage of the trend. Frank Worthing was a great partner, always lending a hand by arranging joint regional sales presentations by our company and MIC.

My relationship with Derrick Draycott and Bruce McDougall had not improved, however. If anything, it had gotten worse. Every time I hired a Genway representative, Draycott was miffed. He truly wanted to see me fail, and my upbeat, positive attitude drove him to distraction – not to mention that the flood of former Genway reps to my operation almost made it seem as if GMAC were supporting the Maguire Agency. Truth be told, WHEELWAYS was riding on GMAC's coattails. Whenever a Maguire agent made a presentation for GMAC, he immediately followed up with a WHEELWAYS pitch.

I ignored the demeaning duo's behavior through the better part of 1973 until I finally got word from Hartford and MIC that Draycott had sent them a broker-of-record letter naming another agent. By that time, Genway had shrunk to a third of its business at its high point, with the other two-thirds being renewed by GMAC. So I viewed the termination as a positive – more time for me to focus on growing my agency.

Goodbye to an Old Friend

No discussion of the Genway years would be complete without remembering Arlette Chellis. Her early role in holding our Philadelphia office together while I structured the Chevway program was invaluable. And during the Chevway years, she maintained all the records on premiums, losses, vehicle penetration, and general behind-the-scenes management.

In 1969, she had suffered kidney failure but was determined to keep working. When I was in Philadelphia, I would visit with her at Temple University Hospital, where she continued her work while she underwent lengthy and frequent dialysis treatments.

Arlette wanted to maintain as normal a life as possible, and her work at the agency was very important to her. By this time, Frannie and I were her devoted friends and would do anything for her – just as she would do anything for us and our family. So it was with great sadness in 1973 that Frannie and I said good-bye to Arlette.

On the cold winter morning of her funeral, we quietly slipped into the last pew at her church, only to be summoned by her brother to come and sit with the family. I was deeply saddened by Arlette's death and was reminded of the things in life that really mattered. Genway, margin calls, GMAC notes, and all the rest seemed very inconsequential.

1974 – A Year that Changed My Life

As we entered 1974 there was great anticipation at home, as we prepared for the arrival of a new Maguire.

Frannie, who was then 38 years old, gave birth to our last child, Tara, who was born on April 10th. Weighing just five pounds, she was beautiful, precious, and tiny! When we brought her home, I offhandedly remarked that she was like a little dew drop. The dew-drop comparison stuck, and ever since, she has been known as Dewey. Although small in stature, our little Dewey would eventually prove that she had the heart of a lion. I was spending more time in Philadelphia by this time and there was a degree of normalcy settling into our home and our life.

I had always understood the inherent disadvantages of developing new products and then having to work with insurance companies to market them, but I viewed it as an occupational hazard. This realization, however, became a painful lesson in the fall of 1974, when Hartford backed out of our exclusive arrangement on the WHEELWAYS program. The normalcy of my life was suddenly turned upside down.

When I opted to place the GMAC lease program with INA, I knew Hartford was disappointed that I didn't favor them with the business.

I also knew that the company's regional offices never liked sending business from their territories through Philadelphia, and I suspected that Draycott and McDougall had poisoned my personal relationship with Hartford's management. WHEELWAYS was a registered trade name so Hartford couldn't use it, but the company could and did sell insurance coverage that mirrored the WHEELWAYS program.

Even though John McCreesh thought I was on unstable ground, I sued Hartford anyway, accusing the company of breach of contract and stealing my intellectual property. Hartford's defense hinged on the fact that our exclusive arrangement was never intended to last forever and had never been formalized with a binding legal agreement.

The case dragged on for months, with depositions taken on both sides, before I realized I couldn't win. When I decided to settle, I ticked off the unpleasant facts: legal bills were mounting; Hartford's lawyers were wearing me down; the depositions were taking time that should have been devoted to running the agency; and my problems with the insurer were of my own doing. I had been naïve in 1970 when I entered into the WHEELWAYS program without spelling out the terms of the partnership. It was time to put the whole unfortunate mess behind me.

I had a business to run and a payroll to meet, so I set out to move the WHEELWAYS program to the Integrity Insurance Company, based in Teaneck, New Jersey.

Integrity, rated A+ by A.M. Best, did most of its business through general agents, had just gone public, and was looking for experienced managing general agents (MGAs). When I visited Integrity's offices, I was directed to Paul Davies, president of Reinsurance Agency Inc., based in Chicago, to secure necessary reinsurance coverage. Thanks to Paul, I hardly missed a beat in switching WHEELWAYS to a new underwriter.

The most exciting part by far was that the Maguire Agency itself would soon be plunging into the risk-bearing and underwriting business, sharing profits or paying losses with Integrity. The risk-bearing partnership was not difficult to comprehend: Premium payments less claims and expense equals underwriting results.

Meeting Paul Davies was an unalloyed stroke of luck. He was well-known in the industry as an expert reinsurance intermediary. If Paul gave his stamp of approval to an agency – as he did to ours after reviewing our numbers and visiting our office to inspect our underwriting and systems capabilities – reinsurers would generally take the account.

The break with Hartford was, without a doubt, the biggest career-changing experience of my life. Although I still owed a portion of the $250,000 promissory note to GMAC, in November of 1974, I put myself and the Maguire Agency on the line and become a risk bearer. I was

embarking on a new career path that would ultimately lead to the purchase of our first insurance company in 1987. There was no hesitation, just my commitment that we would never compromise underwriting standards or pricing to secure business. The day I signed the Integrity contract, I signed a personal guarantee which stood in back of our underwriting agreement. In effect, I bet the farm!!

So far, the decade of the '70s had been a whirlwind of bracing highs and desperate lows – from Hartford's enthusiastic embrace of the WHEELWAYS program to its abrupt decision to sever our ties; from Chevway's stunning early success to Genway's chaotic downfall and the temporary loss of my namesake insurance agency. We had survived an ill-timed margin call, an unfortunate lawsuit, and the assumption of enormous debt. So when I wrote the final check to GMAC in 1976, John McCreesh, my attorney, and I delivered it with pride, in person, over a quiet lunch with Frank Worthing and Tom Patton.

> *The day I signed the Integrity contract, I signed a personal guarantee which stood in back of our underwriting agreement. In effect, I bet the farm!!*

Frannie and I decided to celebrate our debt-free status and renewed ownership of my company by throwing a big party. None of our 80 guests knew the real reason for the grand affair. The event was billed as just a holiday party. Frannie hired a strolling violinist who meandered through the crowd of friends, and a caterer served up an exquisite buffet dinner. Huge baskets of Christmas holly and mixed greens adorned the entire house, the triumph trumped only by my gorgeous Frannie in a flowing white evening gown.

Alicia Wolfington, Shell Morse

Frannie and Jim with Linda and Bob Richenbach

Vince Wolfington and Shell Morse
discussing what could have been!

Frank and Grace Worthing became personal friends. It was
this relationship that helped me grow my business with GM
dealers nationwide.

"The will to win is not nearly as important as the will to prepare to win"

James J. Maguire
Founder, Philadelphia Insurance Companies

Chapter 10

Assembling the Team

▸ **The late 1970s**
WHEELWAYS was nationally recognized as a premier plan.

B
y the mid-1970s, we had 15 offices strategically located throughout the country, with a cadre of independent agents producing a steady flow of business. We were a midsized niche company, writing auto-dealership and leasing and rental insurance.

Amid a wave of government deregulation in the late 1970s, banks won the right to enter the booming car-leasing business. They rushed to compete with finance companies such as GMAC and Ford Motor Credit. As their market share rose, the U.S. Treasury Department's Office of the Comptroller of the Currency (OCC) stepped in with new regulations. In late 1978, OCC issued a memorandum stating that if the unamortized value of a leased automobile exceeded 25 percent of its original cost, the bank had to secure an outside, financially reliable guarantor to relieve the bank of its exposure.

I went to work drafting the first residual value insurance contract for banks, turning to the well-known and highly regarded Automotive Lease Guide (ALG) for help. ALG is an independent company that publishes monthly projections of the future value of every automobile by make, model, and equipment from 12 to 60 months.

I sent the insurance contract and guidebook to the OCC, who confirmed that it complied with the new regulations. I immediately mailed a copy of the confirmation letter to every bank in the country, inviting those that were in or entering the automobile-leasing business to contact our office for insurance coverage. Our sales offices also received the OCC letter with instructions to contact every bank in their territories. What followed was incredible!

Once again the Maguire Agency was at the forefront of the industry, and overnight, a new niche was born.

Sales of residual value insurance came rolling in. As the first and only game in town, we captured most of the eligible banks. Once again the Maguire Agency was at the forefront of the industry, and overnight, a new niche was born. As usual, competitors copied our product – one company even reproduced our policy word for word. But we were the first out of the blocks and comfortably in the lead.

As a companion to residual value insurance, I also introduced a **contingent, or vicarious, liability policy** designed to insure the banks against liability as owner of the leased vehicle. If the lessee was at fault in an accident and had no or insufficient auto insurance, the bank could be held liable. We also offered a service to banks that tracked a lessee's compliance with insurance requirements.

Guaranteed asset protection (GAP) was another first by our agency: insuring a loss, if the vehicle depreciation was greater than the amortized note, at the time of a total loss (usually in the early months of the contract).

The banks' entry into the automobile leasing industry created a new niche, and training our organization was quick and easy. As a result, our representatives were in the field first with a new product to market.

Product innovation was not without its challenges: Along with our success came a level of frustration as I tried to convince insurance companies to underwrite new products like residual value and GAP insurance. Even though we guaranteed the underwriting results, the limited statistical history on the new products made it a challenge to get the issuing company on board. In early 1984, I began to explore the possibility of owning my own insurance company.

Family Snapshots

I was still traveling at least 15 days a month and kept apartments in Chicago and Dallas to serve as jumping-off points for my trips to regional offices in the West and Midwest. Frannie was a near-constant fixture at the children's school and athletic events, and I joined her whenever I could. We coordinated our schedules each Sunday so we could attend as many sporting events as possible, me leaving the office and skipping from football to lacrosse, to tennis and field hockey games. The children took it for granted that we would be cheering them on. Tim once told me that he always knew when I had arrived at his football games because he could hear me cheering from the bleachers. I relished dissecting and rehashing the games with the children afterwards, as my father had taken the time to do with me.

▶ Tara at Penn State
Franny and Tara squared off in a 1993 NCAA
field hockey game.

At one of those games, Tim, who played guard, went down hard. I rushed to the sidelines to hear the team doctor say that Tim's knee was broken. Tim looked at me pleadingly and said, "Dad, tell them to let me finish the game! I'll go to the hospital afterwards."

All the children excelled at sports, and we cheered them on in many a championship game. Our allegiances were severely tested when Tara and Franny faced off in a 1993 NCAA field hockey game. Tara was a Penn State sophomore, and Franny was a senior and captain of the University of Pennsylvania squad. We alternated cheering sections, spending the first half on UPenn's side, and the second half with the Penn State fans. UPenn led one to zero at halftime, but Tara scored three unanswered goals in the second half to secure the victory for Penn State.

When the children had time off from school, we began supplementing our summer vacations in Bermuda with one- or two-week trips to other destinations. Keeping track of eight children ranging from toddler to teenager was an organizational challenge.

▶ Molly Phelan and Franny
Watching Franny grow was beautiful!

Young Franny likes to tell the story of a time in Jamaica when I lined up the family and marched everyone off to a heretofore unexplored private beach about a half-mile from our rented house. As we made our way down an overgrown path, with me looking backward to make sure no one had been left behind, I heard the older kids begin to giggle. It was then that I turned and saw a group of naked people gawking in our direction as the kids gawked right back. We were on a nude beach!

Jamaica was also the scene of another prickly encounter. It was Christmas vacation and we were staying at the Round Hill Resort, just a few miles west of Montego Bay. Megan, then enamored with the violin, decided to perform a solo concert on the beach. Thinking I could do a little snorkeling while listening to her play, I donned my mask and flippers and plunged into the water, which turned out to be much shallower than I expected. With a kick of my flippered foot, I hit a bed of long-spined sea urchins, whose needles pierced my ankle and foot. I reacted by slamming my hands downward to push them away. Very bad move – my hands were covered with spines. "It was the first time in my life that I saw how vulnerable even my 'mighty' father could be," Jamie once said about the incident.

> "It was the first time in my life that I saw how vulnerable even my 'mighty' father could be."
> – Jamie Maguire

Staying Connected in Philadelphia

When Frannie and I married, I was bent on planting roots in Philadelphia, a reaction to my having been uprooted as a youngster and moved from school to school. As our family grew, I became ever more determined to stay involved in the children's schools, our church, local politics, and the business community. I thought it important to give the children a stable environment in which they could establish lasting friendships and future connections.

In the fall of 1979, Frannie and I met Carol and Jim Fitzgerald at the Philadelphia Cricket Club. Both were deeply involved in Philadelphia civic life. Jim was an assistant district attorney in the office of Arlen Specter and was about to run for city comptroller, while Carol worked as the director of alumni relations at the University of Pennsylvania. We would see them at various gallery and museum openings where Carol and Frannie were in their element.

▸ **Fall 1979 - Jim, Carol and Jim Fitzgerald, Frannie**
When Carol and Jim put their collective talent and
determination to a task it would get done!

When Jim decided to run for office, Frannie and I committed to help in any way we could. Our support had nothing to do with party affiliation or making business contacts. We cared about honest government and admired Jim's reputation for integrity. Convinced he was the best man for the job, we invited more than 200 friends, business associates, and politicians, including Pennsylvania Governor Richard Thornburgh, to a fundraiser at our house. The governor, who was in town for an Eagles versus Steelers football game, initially agreed to come for only a few minutes, but he ended up staying for two and a half hours.

It was a spectacular party, complete with buffet dinner, open bar, valet parking, and a passel of prominent people. Perhaps most remarkable was that we hosted some of the brightest stars in Pennsylvania politics that day: Arlen Specter would be elected to the U.S. Senate the following year; Ed Rendell became mayor of Philadelphia and later governor of Pennsylvania; his wife, Marjorie (Midge) Rendell, today is a federal judge.

Though we raised a tidy sum for Jim, he lost the race. But that defeat was only a minor disappointment in a long and distinguished career. Jim subsequently built a successful private practice and served as an executive in the Philadelphia Chamber of Commerce. Then, in 1989, he became a judge in the Philadelphia Court of Common Pleas. Five years later, the state Supreme Court named him the administrative judge of the trial division, overseeing 78 judges and 1,000 employees. In February of 2007, Jim was nominated by Governor Rendell and confirmed by the State Senate to serve on the Pennsylvania Supreme Court.

▶ Fall 1979 - *(left to right)* Jim and Frannie, Arlen and Joan Specter, Carol and Jim Fitzgerald, Midge and Ed Rendell

Arlen Specter was elected a U.S. senator from Pennsylvania. Ed Rendell became mayor of Philadelphia and later served two terms as governor of Pennsylvania. Marjorie (Midge) Rendell was appointed a federal appellate court judge in 1997. Carol Fitzgerald became executive director of the Pennsylvania Society. James J. Fitzgerald III currently serves as a senior judge on the Superior Court of Pennsylvania.

Giving Back

My Jesuit education taught me that we are "men and women for others." Philanthropy has always been an underpinning of my business. Early on, Saint Joe's headed my list of philanthropic causes. Immensely grateful for the opportunities my education had made possible, I gave of my time to the university long before I could afford to make substantial financial contributions. I took an active role in the alumni association, telethons, and other activities, working with Alumni Director Father Michael J. Smith, S.J.

A new institution entered my sight lines in 1973, when my friend Roger Larson, a senior vice president at Sears and a civic leader, called me on behalf of Cabrini College in suburban Philadelphia. Sister Mary Louise Sullivan, president of Cabrini, had told Roger that Cabrini was having financial problems. Roger asked me if I would help.

After a cursory review of the books, I sent accountants from our company to comb through Cabrini's records in preparation for setting up a credit line to forestall future financial emergencies. Thus began more than a decade of involvement with Cabrini.

I was asked to join the college's board of trustees, then made up mostly of nuns and a Jesuit priest, Bill Maloney, who had been president of Saint Joseph's University from 1962 to 1968. The fundraising strategy, if there was one, relied heavily on the notion that God would provide. I shared their faith but thought God wouldn't mind a helping hand from the business community. I started recruiting lay trustees to help put Cabrini back on a solid financial footing. Sister Mary Louise, whose presence, charm, and great empathy captivated me from the start, enthusiastically supported the effort.

In 1974, I was named the board's first lay chairman, whereupon Sister Mary Louise and I began a drastic makeover of the then 287-student women's institution. The first major change was to admit men. Frannie and I started and chaired the Friends of Cabrini Association, which meant that we hosted or arranged dinners and fundraisers. We built new tennis courts and dormitories, the latter to house an influx of out-of-state students. The first of the seven buildings was named the Maguire House.

▶ Jim, Chairman of the Board of Trustees, and Sister Mary Louise Sullivan, President, Cabrini College - 1974

The Cabrini College strategy relied on the notion that God would provide — and I agreed with that. But a little help from the business community, I said, wouldn't hurt.

An important and unexpected dividend from my involvement with Cabrini was developing a friendship with Roger Larson. We first worked together in support of Cabrini in the 1970s, and in 1985, when I began thinking seriously about raising money on Wall Street to buy an insurance company, I asked him to become my first outside director. Besides being smart, competent, and critical when he needed to be, Roger was a financial whiz who helped formulate the capital-raising strategy that underpinned my company's future growth.

Lessons of Loss

None of my siblings had settled in the Philadelphia area, so it was important to me to maintain a relationship with the Maguire side of the family. I felt a special affinity for all of my aunts and uncles on my father's side, but my relationship with Uncle Rab was special. He had been a steady presence in my life: It was Rab who invited me to stay at his and Helen's apartment before and after my father's wake and funeral. It was Rab who came to my college graduation and who

▶ Summer 1978 - Frannie, Tom, and Jim playing gin rummy in Rochester, New York
Following Rab's death, we reconnected as brothers.

In Loving Memory of
ROBERT M. MAGUIRE
Born September 9, 1923
Died February 20, 1978
†
"We have loved him during life; let us
not abandon him, until we have conducted

▶ February 20, 1978
Robert (Rab) Maguire's funeral prayer card.
Our relationship was special.

guided my early career decisions, encouraging me to leave Met Life and strike out on my own. So when Rab died on February 20, 1978, after suffering a heart attack while running, I was devastated. He was only 55 years old, and his death left Helen and their five daughters to make their way without him.

No one would ever replace my father, but Rab had come close. He was my mentor, yes, but also friend, confidant, golf buddy, and running partner. I will always miss him.

All of my siblings came back to Philadelphia for Rab's funeral. The togetherness, coupled with a fresh awareness of the fragility of life, made me value my family – especially my older brother, Tom – in a way I never had before.

Tom and his wife, Mary Ellen, who were raising their eight children in Rochester, New York, had suffered their own tragedy four years before. While hoisting their speedboat out of the water, the motor ran off the rail and severed Tom's right forearm. His blood spurting everywhere, Mary Ellen feared Tom would lose consciousness and die on the dock. Instead, he picked up his arm and walked up a steep hill to the car. Mary Ellen sped to the hospital where Tom's arm

was reattached. He endured several years of rehabilitation and therapy but never regained full use of the arm.

In the years immediately following his accident, I had been consumed with business and lacked empathy for his ordeal. But as he and I mourned Rab's death, pride of place lost its charm, and a brotherly respect took its place.

▶ Jill and Tom Nerney
Courage and leadership exemplified their life.
He had a background and personality similar to mine!

Back to Business

I had resolved to grow the company into a national insurance operation organically. It was my view that acquisitions are expensive and blending cultures is difficult. But as I built the company, our need for talent was also building. To find the right people, I began attending college job fairs where I sought out graduates who had played team sports or had some other type of competitive experience.

Though top academic achievers were certainly welcome, I had come to prize competitive athletic experience even more. Learning about our products was the easy part; having the discipline to prepare, withstand long hours of training, remain loyal to a team, and fight to win against great odds were the qualities that made a businessperson successful. From personal experience, I knew these were the qualities of a good athlete. The euphoria of competing in business is identical to what athletes feel when they've given their all to the game. I had all this in mind when I met and hired Thomas P. Nerney, whom I had the good fortune of meeting through my Cabrini service.

Tom, who came to work for me as a sales representative in 1978, had a background and personality similar to mine. We shared a passion for sports. He was one of Cabrini College's top basketball players and was eventually enshrined in the school's athletic hall of fame. Tom also had an

▶ **Sean Sweeney - I felt that he was my son!**

intense work ethic, an engaging personality, an imposing physical presence with energy to spare, and the distinction of being among the first generation of his family to complete college. Tom was exactly the type of person I wanted to involve in building my company.

The following year, I hired Sean Sweeney, my nephew and scholarship basketball star, who played at Mount Union College in Alliance, Ohio. (Today, the basketball pavilion at Mount Union is known as the Sean S. Sweeney Athletic Center.) Sean and I had always been close, and I loved his competitive spirit – not to mention that we were the Maguire family's only college basketball players (although he was a much better player than I).

Sean and Tom became fast friends, marketing the WHEELWAYS, auto-leasing, and car-rental insurance programs. Sean, who received a competing, $15,000-a-year job offer from Dole Pineapple, has never forgotten the terms and conditions I offered him. I put on the table $12,000 a year, which I described as a pay raise, "and the opportunity to learn the insurance business, work with high achievers, and receive commissions on sales." As an added bonus, I told him he could live rent-free with my mother, Ruth, for a year. Sean concedes that I was right about everything except living with Ruth. "I lasted only seven months," he later told me, "and couldn't take it anymore. If I didn't close the shower curtain in the morning, she'd eat me alive! She was one tough lady."

The euphoria of competing in business is identical to what athletes feel when they've given their all to the game.

The culture I imbued in Sean and the other new recruits included much more than learning the business and selling insurance. Keeping physically fit was a must. The creed I lived by held that you had to be in excellent shape if you wanted to reach and stay at the top of your profession – and there was no room in my company for underachievers. I also insisted that my employees maintain a balance between their business and personal lives; I knew from my own family life that one doesn't work without the other.

I didn't just hire athletes, I raised them. At an early age, I began encouraging my kids to engage in physical activity. Jamie started running with me on weekends when he was eight years old, and the others took to the trails as soon as they were able. As a youngster, Tim wore leg braces to correct his crooked hips, but that didn't excuse him from the family hikes and two-mile runs. When he complained about being tired, I'd grab the back of his belt and lift him a bit to help him make it to the finish line. Quitting was not an option.

> *There was no room in my company for underachievers.*

Running also worked as a disciplinary measure. As a teenager, Susie was a classic push-the-envelope type. On Friday night, I'd give her a midnight curfew and tell her she'd have to run with me on Saturday morning if she was late.

▶ **November 27, 1983 - Susie Maguire's first marathon**
I didn't just hire athletes, I raised them.

▶ **Chris (225 lbs) and Tim (188 lbs)**
Played tackle & guard on their championship high school football teams.

I found myself waking her many Saturday mornings to get her out on the trail. "At first, it was awful," she said, "but Dad knew what he was doing. I started to get into shape and ran my first marathon in 1983. Running also gave me a chance to be together with him one on one."

One Way, Five Rules

Professionalism was one of my main concerns at the agency, and I laid out clear rules to foster it:

1. No drinking on the job.
2. Never be late for a meeting.
3. Don't overspend on the expense account.
4. Surround yourself with winners.
5. Stay physically and mentally fit.

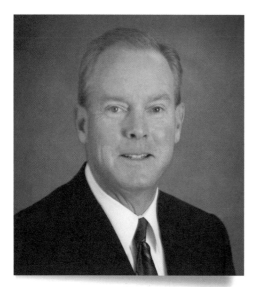

▸ **Robert O'Leary**
Executive Vice President
"Jim got to know our wives and children."

Everyone knew I couldn't stand shortcuts or dishonesty. Bob O'Leary never needed coaching in either. He was a scholarship Trinity College football player and a charismatic leader. I had hired him away from Universal Underwriters, a competitor, to manage the Boston regional office in 1982. I told him not to worry about the money: **"Just show up every day, think about becoming a professional, and the money will take care of itself."**

I kept track of my employees' families as well. "Jim got to know our wives and our children by name," Bob remembers. "If someone was sick or in trouble, Jim was right there or on the phone asking if he could help." Getting to know staff members' families helped to make us a tight-knit organization. When Bob's son, Robbie, came to work for us in the Boston office, I couldn't have been more pleased if he had been my own son. Bob was the first of many employees to bring a second generation to the company.

House Rules

I was having better success establishing and enforcing order at the company than at home. Frustrated by my teenagers' behavior, and inspired by my rules of professional conduct at work, I handwrote a list of house rules in June 1985 and posted them prominently in the kitchen.

The Rules

1. No friends in the house when Mom and Dad are out.

2. Go to church on Sunday.

3. Do not wear others' clothing.

4. Do not enter Mom & Dad's room.

5. Please adhere to our moral code.

6. Please snack in the kitchen.

7. Please use the back stairs after sports.

> *–Dad*

The rules were intended to be serious but lighthearted. Nonetheless, the prescriptions, particularly number five, "adhere to our moral code," reflected my staunch refusal to accept behavior that flew in the face of the values and beliefs Frannie and I had always lived by. One Sunday the boys were dressed for an ice hockey game and were ready to leave when Frannie said they had to go to church first. "God doesn't care what you wear," she told them and off to church she took them in their hockey uniforms.

Back at the office, my hiring pattern rarely varied. I had a sixth sense for finding employees with the qualities I wanted, and I also had a knack for making them want to work for me.

One of my better selections was Chuck Pedone, a strong, gregarious Stroudsburg (Pennsylvania) State College football star who stood an imposing six feet, five inches, and weighed 220 pounds. I had gotten to know Chuck one hot August weekend in 1983, when Susie invited him to the Maryland farm I had purchased three years earlier. He made himself at home and got

▶ **Chuck Pedone**
Vice President: loyalty personified

to work repairing and installing new sections of the four-plank wooden fence surrounding one of the cattle pastures. "It was brutal work," Chuck remembered, "but the highlight of the day was lunch delivered by Frannie from the back of a pick-up truck."

When Chuck graduated from college he contacted me to set up an interview. He arrived 20 minutes late, however, and, mindful of the company rules, I refused to see him. A few years later, Chuck tried again, hoping that I had forgotten the first incident. No such luck. My first words to him were: "At least you got here on time." He joined the company in February 1985.

On October 17, 1989, Chuck, who had been transferred to our San Francisco office, was in Philadelphia for a sales meeting when San Francisco suffered a major earthquake. His wife and family were alone and petrified. Three weeks later, Chuck called to say that our San Francisco office was relocating to Sacramento. He didn't ask if it was okay with me; he simply explained that his wife had said, "Either we move, or I go home to my mother's house in Allentown, Pennsylvania." "Boss," Chuck said, "it's a done deal."

Sean Sweeney, who was named sales manager in 1987, was in charge of hiring and training new representatives. I had devoted a lot of time and effort to grooming my nephew. "If I tried to cut corners in any way," Sean reports, "Jim would be all over me. And when it came time to check the expense reports of the reps in the field, I never forgot the time he made me drive nine hours to Buffalo in a snowstorm just to save the extra money it would cost to fly."

Sean was truly a diamond in the rough when he came to the Maguire Agency. I taught him to present clients with the most complete insurance contract, focusing the presentation on coverage, not price, and doing it with conviction and enthusiasm – though Sean needed absolutely no coaching when it came to his enthusiasm.

Three years into my Sean project and convinced he still possessed an enormous store of untapped raw talent, I decided to give him a leadership role. So, in May 1982, I asked him to open an office in Southern California, somewhere between Santa Barbara and San Juan Capistrano or Laguna Beach.

After surveying the landscape, Sean settled on San Juan Capistrano in Orange County, about halfway between San Diego and Los Angeles. I let him have his head, on the assumption that the business results would confirm or deny the wisdom of his plan. Just as I had hoped, the Maguire Agency's West Coast operations flourished under his leadership. Better yet, he learned firsthand what it takes to open viable offices in previously unfamiliar parts of the country, knowledge that he would use as he led the company's expansion into new cities.

▸ **Robert Pottle**
Senior Vice President
"He was an academic high achiever and All-American track star."

Later that year, I sent Sean to Chicago to interview six job candidates. He called me after the first interview to say he'd canceled the rest. Bob Pottle, a recent graduate of North Central College in Naperville, Illinois, was the man for the job, Sean said. I was more than a little upset, but Sean reassured me by explaining that Bob was an academic high achiever, an All-American track star in the steeple jump, and someone who knew the meaning of discipline, persistence, and hard work.

Sean's instincts proved completely correct. Twenty years later, Bob is a senior vice president and manages 13 offices in the middle of the country, a territory that stretches from Minnesota to Texas. He oversees more than 300 employees, who annually produce over a half-billion dollars of premium income.

Bob's been successful in cloning himself in the people he's hired and the culture he's established. His people show up every day and execute on the business plan with integrity and consistency of purpose. Because he's a winner he has built an organization of winners.

As I continued to recruit top talent from across the country, I found myself thinking more and more about making the next move in the company's evolution. I was about to buy an insurance company.

"Believe what you are and become what you believe"

James J. Maguire
Founder, Philadelphia Insurance Companies

Chapter 11
The Big Leagues

Before · After

▶ 1980 - The Farm

Rebuilding the six-bedroom farmhouse was a labor of love and a lesson in home repair that has served my sons well!

Early in 1980, long before I envisioned buying an insurance company, I made a very different kind of purchase with money I received from the sale of Hav-A-Car, a Philadelphia leasing and rental company that I co-owned with Eustace. We each received $600,000 from the sale to AutoVest, a New York leasing company that Eustace joined after the Genway failure. Given the Maguire Agency's success, I felt free to use my sale proceeds to acquire property in a part of the country that had long beckoned me.

Down on the Farm

During the 1960s, Frannie and I made many trips from Philadelphia to Washington, D.C., to visit my sister Carol, who was then a member of the Sisters of Notre Dame de Namur. As we drove through Maryland, we would often remark on the beautiful, sprawling farms that covered the Chesapeake Bay region. We often wondered who owned these gorgeous properties. Harboring fond memories of the farms and farmers I'd known in my early years, I was inspired to buy a farm of my own. I was captivated by the seeming simplicity of farm life and egged on by daydreams in which my children and I worked the land, cared for the animals, and enjoyed hunting and fishing.

The timing was right. Besides the fact that I had some extra money, our summer routine in Bermuda was becoming untenable. As they grew older the children began to balk at leaving behind their friends, part-time jobs, and various athletic activities. If we bought a farm, I reasoned, the kids could bring their friends with them on weekends.

For six consecutive weekends, Frannie and I drove to Chesapeake City, Maryland, where we looked at dozens of properties before we learned that the 500-acre Elk River Farm was going up for auction. Though severely run down, the property had a mile of waterfront and was only an hour-and-a-half drive from home. It had been subdivided into 11 separate parcels for

▶ **The Farm - After**

500 acres located on the banks of the Elk River, the farm was featured as one of Maryland's premier properties in several local and national publications.

the purposes of the auction, but late in the day, the auctioneer announced that a single bid of more than $550,000 would take the whole thing. I promptly stood up and bought the farm for $600,000, the exact amount I received from the Hav-A-Car sale.

Thus began a three-year renovation project: The barn had holes in the roof, none of the 11 outbuildings had seen paint in many a year, the fences were nothing more than rubber strapping nailed from tree to tree, the pastures were bare from overgrazing, and the dense tangle of bushes, briars, and dying trees totally obscured the view of the river. As for the six-bedroom main house, between nonworking toilets, doors nailed shut, and plastic-shrouded windows, it was unlivable.

Each weekend, our general contractor and I enlisted the boys and some of their friends to help with the dirty work of gutting the house's interior, repairing the outbuildings and fences, and clearing the waterfront. All the buildings were painted white and new red-shingle roofing was laid down.

Intent on making the farm more than a vacation spot, I restored the pastureland and

▶ **Working side-by-side with my sons**
The restoration of the farm was time I cherish. To saddle up and ride the countryside with my daughters is something that bonded my love for them.

▶ **Purebred Angus were recognized as the best of breed.**

bought livestock to graze it. We kept three dozen chickens, 75 head of Black Angus cattle, 75 Cheviot sheep, and 11 horses, including two racehorses that never achieved much success.

Frannie loved the rolling green hills of the Chesapeake and the proximity to Philadelphia, and she did her best to share my enthusiasm for farm life. She even accompanied me to bull auctions. But I was the one who couldn't get enough of the farm. I taught myself to ride a horse, assisted at the birth of calves, helped neuter the bulls, laid out seven miles of post-and-rail fencing that the boys and their friends installed over the course of two years, and tromped around with my chainsaw cutting dead trees and clearing brush. When I wasn't working, I was often hunting.

Though my sons learned invaluable lessons on the farm, they did not always share my enthusiasm for working the land. They quickly became convinced that their sisters got to spend most of their time riding the horses while they did the backbreaking work. It was a conviction their sister Megan pretty much confirmed with her memories of the farm, which run to gauzy mornings spent riding in the countryside and the birth of a foal that I helped deliver.

To improve the boys' experience, I introduced the profit motive, setting up a ranked pay system for them and any of their friends who helped out. "Supervisors" earned the most per hour, "visors" earned slightly less, and "ors" earned the least. Each boy had to earn his rank and promotion in every job, from installing fence to mucking out the barn. "None of us ever served in the Army," Chris once told me, "but that farm was our boot camp." One fall Saturday, Jamie was running the bull calves up a shoot for neutering, when a young bull tried to jump the shoot and hit him, squarely in the face, breaking his nose. With his nose flat against his cheek, he carefully inserted his two little fingers up his nostrils and straightened it out. We all kept working.

An Accident Reawakens Frannie's Talent

Not long after we bought the farm, Frannie was riding her bike around our Chestnut Hill neighborhood early one morning when her rear tire got caught in a trolley track. As she wrenched herself free to get out of the path of an oncoming car, she fell and injured two vertebrae. The first surgical procedure made things worse, leaving her to undergo a second and then a third, followed by months of bed rest and almost two years of rehabilitation.

For the first year after the accident, I would come home from work and bring dinner up to our bedroom so Frannie and I could spend some time together. The kids often brought art supplies to their mother's bedside to help her pass the time.

Frannie's artistic talents began to flourish during her recuperation. As little Franny, nine at the time, remembers, her mother could not engage in much physical activity even as she began to heal, so she returned to painting and sculpting. "We had always known, in an unconscious sort of way," little Franny recalls, "that our mother was a talented artist. But during this period, we saw her in a different way. We realized the extent of [her] talent, interest, experience, and inspiration."

Frannie and I had hoped the farm would provide a safe and structured environment for the children, and, to some degree, it did. But given their ages, farm or no farm, difficult times lay ahead. To this day, Frannie describes those years as "the most challenging times of our marriage."

"We had always known, in an unconscious sort of way, that our mother was a talented artist."

Jamie and Susie were both attending college. Chris, Tim, and Megan were in their teens, and with Franny and Tara were all living at home. Having caused my mother great grief and worry during my high-school years, I began to think that maybe it was payback time.

We usually went to the farm around 3:00 P.M. on Friday and came home late Sunday evening or early Monday morning. As the kids got older, they often tried to get out of going with us. But if they stayed behind, there would be parties and hell-raising at home, and if we stayed at home, there would be parties and hell-raising at the farm.

▸ **University of Pennsylvania field hockey team visits the farm.**

One Friday afternoon, as Frannie and I were driving through Chestnut Hill on our way to the farm, we saw Tim walking out of a beer distributor with a keg on his shoulder. Clearly shocked to see us, Tim put the keg down as he tried to decide whether or not to come over to our car and what he would say once he got there. Meanwhile, the keg started rolling down Germantown Avenue. Despite our anger, we couldn't help laughing.

We spent a wonderful 11 years at Elk River, and it provided a great learning experience. The boys learned how to work with their hands, and we all learned to love and care for animals. These joyful years will long be remembered by our family.

The Last Straw

In the early 1980s, Integrity Insurance Company started to balk at underwriting our new insurance products. I understood Integrity's position when I learned that Mission Insurance Company, its primary reinsurer, was delinquent on approximately $20 million of settled claims. Mission, one of the country's largest reinsurers and rated A+ by A.M. Best, had gotten into trouble when its competitors cut property-and-casualty rates and Mission followed.

Thanks to quick action by my friend Paul Davies, our reinsurance intermediary, we were alerted to Mission's problems early on. With Paul's help, we moved WHEELWAYS and other programs to the Harbor Insurance Company, escaping peril. Nevertheless, as a result of our relationship with Integrity, we, along with every Integrity agent, had to defend against a multimillion-dollar lawsuit filed by the New Jersey Insurance Department before it was eventually dismissed in 1993. By then, the Integrity relationship was a distant memory.

Getting terminated by Harbor was the immediate catalyst that pushed me to buy our first insurance company.

Early in 1985, Ed Hughes, Harbor's president, had asked me to meet him at the New York headquarters of Continental Insurance Company, Harbor's parent company. Dismal results from many of Harbor's managing general agents had led Continental to order it to sever ties with all MGAs, including the Maguire Agency.

I was now faced with the prospect of searching for a new underwriting company at a time when the industry was rife with stories about mismanagement by MGAs.

Getting terminated by Harbor was the immediate catalyst that pushed me to buy our first insurance company. After 26 years in the industry, I was convinced that despite guarantees and letters of credit I could no longer run my company depending on the whims of fronting companies. Bouncing from one insurer to the next, trying to convince them to underwrite the products we developed, was taking its toll in time, money, and energy.

On a warm spring day in May 1986, I brought our management (home office and the 12 regional managers) to a weekend meeting at the farm. I wanted a relaxed setting free of distractions when I unveiled my plan to raise money on Wall Street. We would acquire an insurance company and merge all of our business into the new entity, with the ultimate goal of taking it public. I told the managers they would get stock options in the new company and brashly promised to make them millionaires. In the end, among the excitement and expectations, everyone present pledged their enthusiastic support. This day would prove to be a life-changing event for all 14 managers since all were still employed by the company on the day we went public.

During this meeting I introduced my six-point plan for success.

1. *Business succeeds on professionalism. To that end, we initiated a formal plan of continuing education that encourages advanced academic training, i.e., MBA degrees and CPCU certification. In these continuing education programs, the company would pay 100 percent tuition.*

2. *Winners show up every day. Successful businesspeople, like successful athletes, summon the will to compete every day.*

3. *Passion for the job shores up one's resolve. Without the zealous enthusiasm that defines passion, the drive to succeed is easily derailed.*

4. *Fitness should be viewed as a joy. We strive to hire competitive athletic types and believe that exercising is a great equalizer.*

5. *Surround yourself with winners. Hire like-minded high achievers.*

6. *Maintain a balance between business and personal lives. They feed off each other.*

Though I didn't divulge all the details that day, I had done more than just decide to secure financing for expansion. I had already made a small acquisition that would provide the name and license for the organization of my dreams.

The Box

En route to an insurance convention in Hong Kong the preceding February, Frannie and I found ourselves on the same plane with Paul and Vicky Hertel. Frannie knew Vicky from the Germantown Cricket Club, where both played team tennis. An offhand remark about playing a doubles match led the four of us to meet on the rooftop court at the Hong Kong Hilton.

Following our match, Paul, a rock-solid insurance man who had inherited his father's Philadelphia company, mentioned that he had acquired the Philadelphia Mutual Insurance Company in 1980 as part of a deal to purchase another agency. When the agency piece fell through, Paul was left holding Pennsylvania's first mutual charter insurer (a mutual insurer is owned by its policyholders, not stockholders) and was open to suggestions about what he should do with it.

▶ Tom McHugh

My connection with Tom was serendipitous. He was just starting his own investment firm and I was looking to raise mezzanine financing. We needed each other! Our personalities immediately meshed. Tom was a few years ahead of me at Saint Joseph's University and, like me, he was an athlete. In fact, he had pitched the only no-hitter recorded in Saint Joe's history.

Getting a license as an insurance company in Pennsylvania can be a drawn-out process. I sensed an opportunity. With only two customers, one of whom was Paul, the company was effectively a shell, which meant I could pay out its $100,000 cash surplus to the two policyholders and come away with an insurance-company license. Better yet, the company had "Philadelphia" in its name. By dropping the "Mutual," I would end up with the very name I wanted: Philadelphia Insurance Company.

Upon returning from Hong Kong, I went to Paul's office to retrieve my company and pay $100,000 to him and his partner, Jim McLaughlin, the other policyholder. When the requisite legal documents were all signed, I slid the check across the desk to Paul, who, much to my surprise, pulled a cardboard box from beneath his desk. He thumped the box on the desk and said: "Here's your insurance company." Inside were the license, articles of incorporation, financial statements, convention report, and other applicable paperwork. From that moment on, I referred to the company as "The Box."

I knew, of course, that the company could not accommodate our nationwide insurance business. What I was after, however, was the "Philadelphia" part of my company's name, plus an insurance company licensed in the state of Pennsylvania, and that's what I got. The rest was easy. I filed an application to convert the entity to a stock company and dropped "Mutual" from the name.

A week or so after the meeting at the farm, I contacted Tom McHugh to ask for his help in getting the loan I needed to buy a licensed insurance company. Tom, a Saint Joseph's graduate and somebody I'd known casually, had just formed McHugh Associates, a Philadelphia-based investment advisory company. I was interested in mezzanine financing, which is basically subordinated debt with equity warrants. It's often used to expand an existing company that hopes to go public. Mezzanine financing is a difficult business because many hopefuls never mount a public offering and the payback to the financiers is expensive and can drag on.

While visiting mezzanine lenders with Tom over the next two months, I was told that, typically, a would-be borrower identifies a target company before seeking financing. The prospective financiers all wanted to see my target's financial structure. Instead, I said, "Give me the money first, and then I'll find the right company." It was a little like securing a mortgage without yet having chosen a house. My theory was that too many guys were looking for an acquisition without having the money to do a deal. With the money in hand, I would have much more credibility and bargaining power.

▸ **Rohit Desai**
Rohit was smart and financially detail oriented. The lessons learned while dealing with him proved invaluable as I prepared to enter the public arena.

When the investors asked me for my business plan, it was financially solid yet simple: Move my existing agency business which had a combined ratio of 90 percent, into my own insurance company. Steady growth had brought us to about $65 million in gross premiums, and if we continued our disciplined underwriting and pricing approach, I felt sure that an $18 to $20 million loan would be enough to support our business.

Finally, Rohit Desai, the general partner of Equity-Linked Investors, agreed to do the deal. The completed financing package included $11 million from my old standby, First Pennsylvania Bank, in the form of 8½ percent senior debt. The remaining $8 million was subordinated debt backed by Maguire Agency stock and personally guaranteed by Frannie and me. The debt carried a 10 percent coupon and included warrants to purchase 25 percent of the company's common stock in a public offering. One-eighth of the debt was held by McHugh Associates and the remainder by Rohit Desai's company.

Desai was a slightly built, stern, and serious businessman of Indian descent who watched our finances like a hawk and expected projections to be carefully thought out and met. And rightly so, since the payoff for Equity-Linked Investors lay in the warrants, the value of which depended on the success of a public stock offering.

Although the terms of the financing were stiff, the process of obtaining it was one of the great learning experiences of my life. I admired Rohit's focus on business and appreciated everything he taught me about becoming a public company: The detailed reporting procedures required by Wall Street; the quarter-to-quarter comparisons of premium growth, earnings, return on equity, book value, and so forth; the need for annual budget projections and the importance of meeting them; detailed explanations of any missteps – all these things and more became standard operating procedure for us after closing the debt financing on October 20, 1986.

The Perfect Company

While I had been raising capital on Wall Street, my good friend Dick Stout had been shopping for an insurance company I could buy. Dick was a well-connected business broker whom I had known for 15 years. A sweetheart of a man, he never failed to ask about Ruth after he happened to meet her one day when he stopped by my office. "Are you taking good care of Ruth?" he'd always ask.

Dick specialized in buying and selling insurance companies and he came up with several possibilities. But it was the Preserver Insurance Company that caught my eye. It was owned by a French bank, licensed and bonded in 33 states, rated A+ by A.M. Best, had no long-tail exposure (meaning there was no risk of claims being filed long after policies expired), no open regulatory investigations, and a $28 million claim reserve. Preserver also had $25 million in gross premiums (mostly auto physical damage) and had earlier initiated a runoff of that business, leaving only four months of in-force policies. Dick had dissected and laid out every pro and con.

Indeed, Dick walked me through every phase of the purchase: what to ask for, what to reject, how to establish a contingent claim fund, and, most important, what to pay. So when Dick and I met with the French bank owners and their attorneys in New York at 9:00 A.M. on August 20, 1987, they quickly realized that I had done my homework. By 2:30 that afternoon, we had a handshake agreement, and within 45 days, I owned the Preserver, which I renamed the Philadelphia Indemnity Insurance Company.

My first major decision as the company's owner concerned the management. After spending time with the senior officers, I decided they didn't fit with our culture, and I terminated them. Shortly thereafter, I visited A.M. Best headquarters in Oldwick, New Jersey, and introduced myself as the new CEO. I identified Tom Nerney and Sean Sweeney as the executive vice presidents and said the former management had been terminated.

What happened next shocked me. My company's A+ rating was revoked. The people at A.M. Best explained that since I had never owned or operated an insurance company, Philadelphia Indemnity would be designated N.R., "not rated." I was dumbstruck! My years in the business, my knowledge of underwriting and pricing, my policy filings – none of it counted for anything. They said my only option was to retain the existing management for a minimum of three years, during which time I was supposed to learn from them how to run an insurance company. I asked Best to give me a week to think it over.

When I got back to Philadelphia, I met with the ex-president of Preserver, who volunteered that he and his executive vice president would be glad to stay on as the executive officers for three years. They'd sign the annual convention statements and any other required documents. I felt uncomfortable with the arrangement, however. I wanted to start my insurance company with a clean slate.

I reluctantly accepted Best's N.R. rating for three years and promoted Tom Nerney to the post of chief operating officer. Since coming to the company in 1978 he had become a student of the business with boundless energy. Together, we set out to solve the problem of owning an unrated insurance company licensed in 33 states.

Answering the Call at Saint Joe's

Having served as a Cabrini trustee for 14 years, I felt it was time to resign from the board. Sister Mary Louise Sullivan had stepped down as president in 1982, and the college had successfully

▸ **Fr. Nick Rashford, S.J.**
President of Saint Joseph's University (1986-2003).
He oversaw a major expansion of the university.

become a co-educational institution with seven new residence halls. The dire financial condition that drew me to the school in the first place was stabilized and the budget was balanced.

My support for Saint Joseph's University had never waned over the years, and when Father Nicholas Rashford, S.J., approached me about joining the board of trustees in 1988, I accepted. Thus began an exciting four-year tenure that ended in the summer of 1992 when I resigned to focus my attention on preparations to take my company public.

Father Nick, who was inaugurated as Saint Joe's 25th president in 1986, was a big, energetic, and ambitious man. He had a vision for Saint Joe's and would not be deterred. Nick oversaw a major expansion of the university that added new dormitories and a multimillion-dollar academic facility with a fully networked communications center. He brought Saint Joe's into the 21st century. He also added master's degree programs in several disciplines.

I chaired the capital campaign that built the Michael J. Smith, S.J., Memorial Chapel, named after a dear friend and one of the most beloved Jesuits in Saint Joe's history. The chapel dedication in May of 1992 was a beautiful and moving affair, presided over by Anthony Cardinal Bevilacqua. In the vestibule of the chapel stands a bronze bust of Father Mike that had been sculpted by Frannie.

Mike had traveled through Ireland with us and Father Nick during the summer of 1989. He suffered a heart attack and died just six months after our return. When he was discovered slumped over his desk, there was a half-penned letter to Frannie beside a box of Irish cookies she had sent him.

In 2003, following Fr. Rashford, came Fr. Timothy R. Lannon, S. J., as the 26th president of the university. Although not on the board of trustees, I was privileged to work with him in the acquisition of the adjacent 38-acre Episcopal Academy, which is now known as the "James J. Maguire '58 Campus." During Tim's tenure, he initiated a $150 million capital campaign which enabled tremendous improvements in student housing, the Campus Student Center, and the basketball facility, now known as the Michael J. Hagan '85 arena.

▶ Dedication of Michael J. Smith, S.J., Memorial Chapel 1992

(left to right) Tim, Jim, Fr. Nick Rashford, S.J., Frannie, Megan Maguire Nicoletti, Anthony Cardinal Bevilacqua, Chris, and Mark Nicoletti. Frannie sculpted the bust of Fr. Mike Smith.

▶ September 2008 - Dedication of the Maguire Campus

Fr. Tim Lannon, S. J., President, Frannie, The Honorable Michael A. Nutter, Mayor of Philadelphia, and Jim

Father Lannon also played a significant role in boosting the university's academic standards, including new endowed faculty chairs, student scholarships, revised and improved undergraduate curriculum, opening of a Center for Business Ethics, a Center for Autism Education and Support, and the Academy of Risk Management and Insurance, which I chair.

"Show up every day, opportunity will come"

James J. Maguire
Founder, Philadelphia Insurance Companies

Chapter 12
Shaping the Philadelphia Insurance Companies

▶ Roger Larson

I trusted his advice and sought his counsel before I made business decisions. He was a prince of a man.

▶ Eustace Wolfington

Eustace was a great friend from my days at Saint Joseph's University. He was a recognized visionary in the automobile leasing and rental business and a world-class marketing executive.

▶ Paul Hertel, Jr.

Paul recommended I surround myself with talented and experienced board members.

I ncorporating Philadelphia into the new company's name was a deliberate decision. Maguire Insurance Agency had been fine for a time, but Philadelphia Insurance suggested more: history, continuity, size, dependability, even a certain refinement. I always pay attention to details and knew that choosing the right name for the company was no small matter.

I also knew the importance of surrounding myself with talented and experienced board members. Paul Hertel had emphasized that fact not long after he sold me his insurance company. The financing agreement dictated that Tom McHugh and Rohit Desai take board seats, and I could choose three independent directors to join them. Heeding Paul's advice, I initially invited Roger Larson, Eustace Wolfington, and Paul himself.

I selected Paul for his experience and insider's understanding of the insurance industry – his grandfather had started the family's insurance brokerage in 1908. Paul had also served as chairman of the Excelsior Insurance Company.

Eustace was invited because I wanted the benefit of his marketing experience, plus I needed a sounding board, not a yes-man.

I chose my friend Roger, now retired from Sears, because of my relationship with him during and after the Cabrini College crisis. He had shown himself to be a smart, fair, and hard worker. In his new role on the Philadelphia Insurance board, Roger prodded me to think about the future and insisted that I have a rolling five-year business plan. He also encouraged me to visit Wall Street to learn about public financing.

Although I did not intentionally stack the board with friends, the same could not be said for the company. Just as I had done in 1964, when I hired Ruth to corral the agency's delinquent customers, I welcomed – actually sought out – family members to help me run the new business. I had enormous confidence in their work ethic and loyalty to me and the enterprise we would build.

▶ **Sean Sweeney and Jim (Ellen Larson -background)**
Sean receives congratulations at the Bermuda National Sales Conference. His leadership was an important reason for our success. The Sales-Trac system guaranteed success, and "10 Reasons Why" on each product set us apart from competitors.

Sean Sweeney proved my instincts correct. Each year, my nephew's abilities shone brighter. Organized, creative, and 100% loyal, I promoted him to senior vice president and chief marketing officer after I completed the financing. He immediately got busy installing the Sales-Trac system that we still use today. It assures quality submissions and complete information, while identifying price shoppers and showcasing the differences between our products and those of competitors.

Sean's success only deepened my desire to have my sons in the company, so I was delighted when Jamie joined us in 1986.

Jamie started his college career with a brief stay at the University of Richmond and then transferred to Georgetown University. "A little too much fun," as he describes it now, took a toll on his grades. Just as I had done with Tim and Chris when their grades slipped, I put Jamie to work. He spent a year in the Hav-A-Car leasing operation as a car jockey and gofer. Lesson learned, he enrolled at Saint Joe's and earned a bachelor's degree in 1984, then went on to Notre Dame's MBA program in the fall. There, he compiled a 4.0 GPA.

Jamie had specialized in commodities trading while pursuing his master's and considered working in Chicago on one of the exchanges – until he realized how much he wanted to return to Philadelphia. He started in our marketing department, but within a few months we put him in charge of our new financial products division, which he helped to develop. We designed a complete, very specialized package of products for banks, including Directors and Officers (D&O) liability, mortgage-impairment coverage, and a banker's blanket bond. Trade-named BANKWAYS, it was a success largely because of Jamie's ability to evaluate the financial information that underlay the division's underwriting activities.

The End of an Era

My 30-plus years in the insurance industry had taught me that products have a finite shelf life. New ideas and offerings can't be copyrighted, and new competitors will often cut prices to gain market share.

As the year 1988 progressed, increasingly intense competition for auto-dealership business was driving down prices. I had no intention of giving into it.

Worse, the time spent quoting and re-quoting dealership accounts was hurting productivity. Sean, who was on the West Coast competing for business, quoted 21 accounts without a single sale over a three-month period. He called me and said we had to do something. "I now know how the Red Coats felt during the Revolutionary War," he said. "Everyday I go out and get shot down!" We were losing business and valuable time trying to hold onto existing accounts.

Company morale was low, and our agents all across the country were complaining that competitors were undercutting our prices. My answer never varied: If others are stupid, that's no reason for us to be stupid.

▸ **August 1988 - National sales meeting - Bermuda**
(left to right) Mary Ellen O'Leary, Jim, Chuck Pedone, Kay Desai.
There was discussion and tension about cancelling WHEELWAYS.

My 30-plus years in the insurance industry had taught me that products have a finite shelf life.

We were running in place, though. Our WHEELWAYS revenue was decreasing even as we stepped up our efforts to keep the business going. Despite processing twice the number of quotations, year-over-year, premium income shrank. Forced to re-quote our renewal price two or even three times, we got closer to zero profit with each subsequent reduction.

Since introducing WHEELWAYS through the Hartford in 1970, I'd had to change issuing companies three times. Each move was tedious, time-consuming, expensive, and logistically challenging. My original plan was to move all business generated by the Maguire Insurance Agency into our new company. But with the dealership business shrinking and profit margins narrowing, terminating WHEELWAYS and preserving our capital for more promising lines of business seemed to be the only choice.

Eustace, Paul, and Roger understood my predicament and agreed with me that there was no way to predict when the underwriting cycle would turn around. Companies were competing at reduced rates just to get the investment income – a risky ploy known as cash-flow underwriting – and I was unwilling to compete on that basis.

Not everyone on the board seconded my assessment, however.

From the beginning, I'd known that Rohit Desai was particularly keen to track monthly and quarterly results. Sitting on the board allowed him to keep tabs on his investment. Now he was furious that I would even consider getting out of WHEELWAYS. Given that he and Tom McHugh were my chief financial backers, their opposition was understandable. They reminded me that when they agreed to the financing, WHEELWAYS was what IPO investors would find attractive. When I held firm, Rohit responded by proposing (threatening) to change the terms of the finance agreement to include a buyout of the warrants. It was a move he would later regret. Reassuring our sales force was no easy task, either. "What will we do? What will we sell? Will you subsidize our income?"

Even my friend Bob O'Leary, who headed our Boston operation, was apprehensive. Bob realized that jettisoning WHEELWAYS and striking out in a new direction would be a tough transition for many people but absolutely necessary to ensure our long-term viability. Still, he feared the loss of a strong group of salespeople who had spent years building dealer relationships. He himself had two children and was nervous until his wife reminded him that "Jim has eight kids, and he isn't panicking!"

I brought the management together for two days in April 1989 to talk about the move, explaining my reasoning and laying out my long-range plans. "We will develop new niche products, but more importantly, just show up every day, and the rest will take care of

▸ **April 1989 - Management meeting -**
termination of WHEELWAYS
WHEELWAYS was a major reason for our growth
and national recognition.

itself," I said. They still weren't convinced. That's when my legendary temper flared. I stood up, slammed my pad on the table, and said, "If one more person in this room says something negative, I am going to punch him."

Bluster and threats aside, I wanted my staff to understand my personal philosophy:

Just show up every day and the rest will take care of itself.

My point that day was that WHEELWAYS was over. The good news was that the runoff process wouldn't deplete our WHEELWAYS income all at once, plus we had $19 million in the bank to tide us over while we reinvented ourselves. Why waste another minute? We needed to get busy creating our next success.

No Niche Left Behind

My plan was straightforward. First, we would redouble our efforts to sell primary liability and physical damage coverage to car-leasing and rental accounts. More banks were getting into leasing, and we could also go back to smaller rent-a-car operations and recreational-vehicle accounts that were never contacted.

Second, I challenged our managers to become more entrepreneurial and come up with niche-product ideas that could be presented to our product development committee. I also asked them to solicit ideas from the brokers with whom we were doing business.

Third, Sean, who introduced the Sales-Trac system, added a list of "Ten Reasons Why" Philadelphia Insurance was better on each product sold, and it became part of every sales presentation with a highlight sheet attached.

Eight of our top salespeople couldn't adapt to the loss of WHEELWAYS and left the company. I was hurt when they resigned but we had to move on.

Rohit Desai couldn't adapt, either. He simply could not accept my underwriting decision. In his mind, I was a creditor, and he was furious that my previous projections were no longer valid. I had hoped and expected that the soft market would run its course and business would start to improve. When that didn't happen, the risk of continuing became, in my opinion, too great.

Tough as Rohit was, I wasn't cowed by his fury. I knew the insurance business and understood that when a line of business went bad you had to get out; Rohit's inability to comprehend the changing market caused him to lose confidence in me. In June 1989, I finally pulled the plug on WHEELWAYS, and we began the runoff.

Still fuming, Rohit proposed that I buy back the warrants included in the lending deal that gave holders the right to purchase 25 percent of the company's common stock in an IPO. He again argued that the mezzanine financing was done on the assumption that WHEELWAYS would be an enticement to Wall Street in a public offering. Shutting it down made the warrant holders feel misled, he said, and now they wanted Philadelphia Insurance to buy out their warrants at $1,524.97 for each $1,000 note tendered.

I was never very happy giving up warrants for a fourth of our company in the first place, so when he proposed that I buy them back, even at the steep redemption price, I was glad to accommodate him. In October 1989, I signed the agreement and bought back the warrants.

Thereafter, Rohit lost interest in the company, particularly in helping me with an IPO. He even stopped attending board meetings. Fortunately, the same was not true with Tom McHugh. He remained active as a board member and told me if the company was any good (as I knew it was) Wall Street would figure that out and compete for the business. As far as I was concerned, it was never a matter of whether the company would go public, it was just a matter of when.

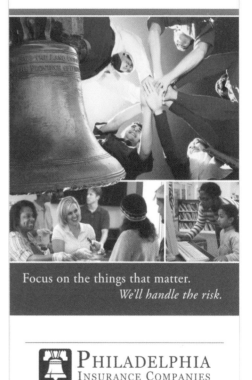

Non-Profit and Social/Human Services Package

Focus on the things that matter.
We'll handle the risk.

PHILADELPHIA
INSURANCE COMPANIES

▸ **The product development committee**
Introduced insurance for the Social/Human Services industry in 1989. When George H.W. Bush, our 41st president, gave his "thousand points of light" inaugural address, we were in the market and ahead of the industry.

Light Shines on a Profitable New Niche

On January 20, 1989, George H.W. Bush addressed the country for the first time as the 41st president of the United States. In that inaugural address, he returned to a theme he had first broached when he accepted his party's presidential nomination. "I have spoken of a thousand points of light," he said, "of all the community organizations that are spread like stars throughout the nation, doing good. We will work hand in hand, encouraging, sometimes leading, sometimes being led, rewarding ... I will go to the people and the programs that are the brighter points of light, and I will ask every member of my government to become involved ...."

Thus began a reassessment of nonprofit social-service agencies and organizations in the United States. The Bush administration opted to reduce the federal government's role in providing social services, instead funding nonprofit initiatives such as homeless shelters, soup kitchens, battered women's shelters, drug and alcohol rehabilitation centers, and other privately run, tax-exempt programs. This was a major turning point for our company.

> *Once again we had found success by being at the forefront of our industry.*

We had begun to explore opportunities in the nonprofit sector as we were winding down WHEELWAYS. One of our underwriting managers had some previous experience underwriting nonprofits and introduced the idea during one of our many new-product meetings. Our test marketing was already showing great promise when President Bush took up the cause. We were perfectly positioned to move quickly into this niche with property, liability, and vehicle coverage. Then, when the nonprofits began recruiting board members to help manage the local agendas and government subsidies, we offered them Directors and Officers (D&O) liability coverage. Later, we added other types of coverage based on the recommendations of our field people and agents. In short order, we became the best, most comprehensive insurer of nonprofit social-service agencies in the country. Once again we had found success by being at the forefront of our industry, anticipating the needs of our clients and delivering the best possible product.

Steve Westhead from Kansas City called me at home one Friday evening. He had just met with the executive director of the International Union of Gospel Missions, a Kansas City-based

Christian organization that operated homeless shelters and soup kitchens. Some 8,000 missions were sprinkled around the country, and they were paying exorbitant prices for inadequate property, liability, and vehicle insurance. He thought the missions qualified for standard-risk policies. "There aren't many situations where lawyers are going to feel good about suing a gospel mission in a distressed area," he theorized.

He sounded apologetic for bothering me at home with a prospect he hadn't yet fully validated, but reaching out to prospects overlooked by our competitors was exactly what I wanted. It was a formula that served me well from my earliest days in the business, when I convinced Met Life to offer equal treatment to deaf policyholders. "You may be onto something," I replied. "Who else would insure a soup kitchen?"

I flew to Kansas City the following week to meet the mission director. We agreed to insure their 8,000 missions, but not without some operating changes. I insisted that all drivers have accident-free records and complete a driver training course, and, also, that implementation of safety initiatives were prerequisites for property coverage. The director didn't object. He was eager to put the missions on a safe and sound footing.

The extraordinary success of the Gospel Missions program made it the model in our pursuit of other niche markets.

Pumping Up Business with Health Clubs

With Tom and Sean handling most of the day-to-day operations and marketing for the company, I was free to concentrate on uncovering our weaknesses and looking for more niche markets. The product development committee, which met each month, followed up its introduction of nonprofit D&O liability with **a package for health and fitness clubs**, a market segment that was a natural fit for a company with a fitness culture like ours.

As with all new niche ideas, we test marketed health-club insurance in several regions to find out what we needed to know and to study competitors' offerings. We discovered that there were 30,000 fitness clubs nationwide, each paying an insurance premium that typically ran below $25,000. So competition was limited, the business carried no long-tail exposure, and the distribution of fitness clubs nationwide meant that each of our offices would have its own customer base.

As with every new-product idea, we found 10 ways to differentiate our program from what competitors were offering.

We've made a point, for example, never to turn away small customers. We treat the small battered-women's shelter with its $20,000 premium just as we would a million-dollar Salvation Army contract. In the case of the health and fitness program, we separated ourselves from the crowd and won the gratitude of the fitness industry simply by adding malpractice coverage for trainers. Until then, if a fitness trainer instructed a client on how to lift weights, let's say, and the client got hurt, the trainer – and by extension, the fitness facility – could be liable. Our policy broke the mold by offering protection for both.

I was also paying close attention to outside forces. I visited A.M. Best semi-annually pleading my case in hopes of securing a rating before 1991. It never happened, forcing us to pay a 3 percent fee to have our policies issued through A+ rated North American Specialty Insurance Co.

Family Arrivals

My son Chris, who had been a part-time trainee each summer since January of 1987, joined the company in 1989 after graduating from Villanova. Chris began working in the underwriting department.

Having my children work for the company was something I had long imagined as idyllic. The reality was something else, however. Tim, who had yet to finish college, was working part-time and wasn't serious about anything, bouncing from the mailroom to claims to inside sales. "I still had a lot of growing-up to do," he admitted later. Chris, however, liked the underwriting department from the start and was an exceedingly quick study. But he and I had some philosophical differences to iron out.

Chris had to learn my philosophy about underwriting: you never write bad business to get good business. I expected that each segment of an account had to produce an underwriting profit. But Chris, who was working in our Rent-A-Car program, added together the profitable auto liability with the unprofitable auto physical damage to come up with an overall acceptable loss ratio for an account.

Chris had to learn my philosophy about underwriting: you never write bad business to get good business.

I told him to raise the physical damage rates so the line would be profitable. He argued that he'd lose the whole account. I told him to do it anyway. Over the next six months, he successfully raised the physical damage rates and both lines of Rent-A-Car started making money.

But Chris's learning curve was nothing compared to the blow Jamie delivered the previous year, 1988. I was aware that he had never felt entirely comfortable at Philadelphia Insurance. The situation worsened in 1987 when I named Tom Nerney executive vice president and chief operating officer and made Sean a senior vice president.

It was a Friday night in October. Frannie and I had just finished dinner when Jamie and his wife, Lisa, arrived unannounced. "What brings you down here this chilly night?" I asked as I stood to kiss Lisa. Without any small talk or clue as to what was coming, Jamie blurted, "Dad, I'm leaving the company and won't be back on Monday."

I was shocked. For a moment, I couldn't believe what I was hearing. Then a crushing wave of emotion rolled over me, and I fell back into my chair as tears filled my eyes.

Had I done something wrong? Had I been too tough? Did Jamie want a firmer commitment concerning his future at the company? Was the stumbling block money? Position? Conflict with the management team?

> *(left to right)* **Jamie, Jim, Sean Sweeney, Susie, Tom Nerney, Pete Resch**

My thoughts raced. How could I salvage my dream of having my sons take over Philadelphia Insurance one day? Bringing Jamie into the company had created a delicate situation. I couldn't designate him, or any of my sons for that matter, as heir apparent before I knew what they could do, and I certainly didn't want to alienate my management team by showing favoritism. Instead, I had decided to let Tom, Sean, and my sons work together as a team.

> ▶ **October 1987 - Jamie finishing half-marathon**
> He vowed it would never happen again!

I was baffled when Jamie told me he didn't have another job – hadn't even been looking for one because he thought it wrong to do so while he was working at Philadelphia.

I thought back to an incident that might have led him to think he would be more comfortable working somewhere else. Tom, Sean, Susie, Pete Resch, and I had trained together to prepare for a half-marathon in Philadelphia. At the last minute, Jamie, who had only recently joined the company and hadn't done any training for the race, decided to run with us.

We completed it easily in under an hour and 40 minutes. Jamie, who ended up having to walk the last four or five miles, arrived at the finish line long after the other runners had finished. Everyone insisted it was no big deal, but given the competitive spirit I had fostered in the family, it was clearly a difficult experience for him.

"What could I do differently?" I asked.

"Nothing," he said.

Just as I had always discussed matters with Frannie, Jamie had spent hours talking with Lisa over the previous month, and his mind was

▸ Sean and I had a father-son relationship

He was receptive and eager to learn and had a competitive spirit like nobody else I've ever coached. Sean's success was PHLY's success!

made up. He saw no reason to go into specifics, saying only that he needed a change, an opportunity to carve out his own path and make a name for himself in the industry – something he thought he could never do working in his father's shadow.

Later, Jamie would say that he had inherited an "independent gene" from me, always wanting to do things on his own. What pushed him over the edge I'll probably never know. Maybe it was a feeling that his interests were not in sync with the company overall. Maybe he wanted to sharpen his mastery of professional liability products, which demanded more quantitative analysis and subjective thinking in the underwriting process. It was the kind of work he enjoyed.

Thanks to Frannie's counsel, I was wise enough to give Jamie the space and time he needed. Having always known the value of silence, its healing power and ability to let people regain their composure and collect their thoughts, Frannie understood Jamie's reluctance to talk at that difficult moment.

Jamie was unemployed for five months, and it was not an easy time for either him or Lisa. After Jamie returned his company car, they had to share their Subaru pickup truck. Lisa, who was also unemployed at the time, decided to take over a paper route, delivering *The Philadelphia Inquirer*. Working from 2:30 till 6:00 each morning, she brought a little cash into the house and was back home before Jamie even woke up. When Jamie decided to join Lisa in the venture, it meant that two Notre Dame MBAs were handling one paper route – not quite what anyone imagined on graduation day in South Bend.

Later that year, Jamie joined the CNA Insurance Company in Chicago, eventually making professional liability insurance his specialty. As his career blossomed, Frannie and I were proud and happy. Whatever breach might have existed was repaired, and in 1990 we visited Jamie and Lisa to watch him run the Chicago Marathon. This was the start of a pleasurable pastime that eventually took him to multiple marathons and Ironman competitions, two of which were in Hawaii.

Jamie and I talked often about the accounts he was insuring and his career as he climbed the ladder at CNA, then Great American, and, finally, AIG. He rose to become an assistant vice president at AIG, gaining confidence, earning respect from professional underwriters, and benefiting from learning experiences not available at Philadelphia Insurance. During the course of this journey, he became his own man—proving perhaps that all along he had known better than I did what was best for him. I recalled my own need for independence when I left Met Life at the start of my career.

Nevertheless, I wasn't relinquishing my dream. I was biding my time till the day I could entice my eldest son to return to Philadelphia Insurance.

▶ Jamie completes 2005 Ironman

Wall Street Journal names him CEO Athlete of the Year.

"Integrity: Adherence to a strict moral and ethical code"

James J. Maguire
Founder, Philadelphia Insurance Companies

Chapter 13
Going Public

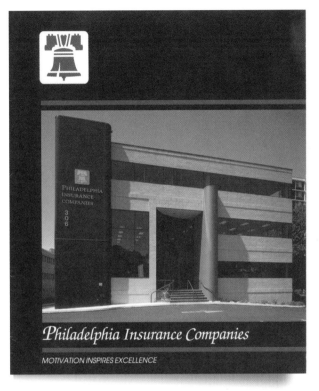

▶ **Home office 1989-1996**

With Rohit Desai out of the picture, I needed to find someone else to champion my plans for going public. It was then I realized I was on my own and I'd have to be my own champion. In April 1990, with coaching from Tom McHugh, I planned my first visit to Wall Street. I was unsure about what to expect, but as always, I put on a positive front. Tom agreed to go with me, and through his contacts, set up several appointments.

Making the rounds on Wall Street was a great education. The people I met were friendly and liked the story I had to tell – as much of it, that is, as I could convey in the short time allotted to me. But everyone I spoke to – bankers at Prudential Securities; Schroeder & Company; Donaldson, Lufkin & Jenrette (DLJ); Goldman Sachs; Merrill Lynch; and Legg Mason – said we were a little too small to go public.

My second trip to Wall Street was more encouraging: DLJ's senior vice president for insurance banking, Pedro Galban, had asked me to stay in touch.

I already knew Pedro from my days of doing business with the now-defunct Integrity Insurance, where he had held a position on the company's board. Pedro listened to my half-hour presentation and reviewed our financial statements. Then he and his assistant, Jim Zech, took me to lunch in DLJ's executive dining room. Their message: If Philadelphia continued to grow at its current pace, the company could be a candidate for a public offering by 1993, and asked that I send our three-year projections (1993 was an important year since the mezzanine financing was callable in October).

▶ **1991 - Paul Hertel and Tom McHugh**
Annual board meeting in Bermuda.

Toward the end of 1992, the IPO market started to heat up. With 20 percent year-over-year growth the previous two years, Philadelphia Insurance had become a prime candidate for an offering. I had stayed in touch with Pedro and Jim, providing them with updated financial information. But when I visited Pedro late in the year, I learned that, because of the high volume of IPOs, DLJ had arbitrarily set a minimum of $100 million on offerings the firm would take to market. Pedro said it was more than we could justify.

Jim Zech had recently left DLJ to head up S.G. Warburg's new insurance division for mergers and acquisitions, and Pedro suggested I contact him since Warburg was entertaining smaller deals. Under pressure to make something happen and do some deals at his new company, Jim was initially excited to see me and seemed eager to explore an IPO. To my frustration, however, he thought that combining Philadelphia with another insurance company would make an IPO more appealing to investors.

I had vetoed merger suggestions before beginning my Wall Street conversations because of my concerns about blending management and different cultures. Any larger partner would want to control us, and smaller companies were not worth bothering with. To me, the potential downside of such a merger far outweighed any upside.

A Break in the Logjam

Late in 1992, I contacted Richard Nager, a New York banker at Josephthal & Company. Nager had just completed an IPO for a Philadelphia telemarketing company, and I invited him to come hear the Philadelphia Insurance story. To my surprise, he spent an hour telling me what I needed to do – after disqualifying his own company as too small to do a deal with us. Nager approved of my dealings with Warburg but encouraged me to bring in a second firm. Competition is always good, he said, particularly if I didn't want to pursue the merger Jim Zech was pushing. "Contact the Chicago Corporation," Nager told me, "they're looking to do deals."

In late February 1993, our new chief financial officer, Craig Keller, sent our year-end 1992 numbers to both Warburg and Chicago along with our pro forma five-year projection, assuming $50 million of new capital. One month later, on April 13, Chicago Corp. came calling, intent on learning everything they could about us. At the end of the visit, they declared us an ideal candidate for an IPO, and one with whom their company would welcome the opportunity to work.

> *Our offering would eventually be consummated at a heretofore unimagined 19 times earnings.*

Meanwhile, Jim Zech hadn't given up on the idea of increasing the size of our deal through a merger. But when I told him that Chicago Corp. liked our company, he invited Craig and me to come to New York to meet with other Warburg bankers. The Warburg meeting went off without a hitch, and the merger idea fell by the wayside.

In the early '90s, investors couldn't seem to get their fill of new stock offerings, snapping up everything in sight at substantially high prices. Buyers once willing to pay only seven or eight times earnings for insurance company deals were now bidding two and a half times that amount. Our offering would eventually be consummated at a heretofore unimagined 19 times earnings.

Anxious to take advantage of the hot market, Jim Zech asked for an April meeting at Philadelphia with Chicago Corp. At that gathering, he committed to an IPO, presented a calendar of things to do, and set the date to go public. It was a done deal.

Taking the Show on the Road

The last point of discussion between the bankers concerned who would travel where during the road show. Warburg wanted to take the lead at every stop, but Chicago Corp. managed to wrest control in locales where their firm had a strong presence. Tom Nerney, Sean, and I were asked by Jim Zech to put together a 25-minute presentation on the company for the road show.

We did our best, but when Jim came to Philadelphia to view the finished (we thought) product, he wasn't happy. A week later, he was back with his own version of how our story should be told.

▸ Jim Zech

Jim left DLJ to head S.G. Warburg's insurance division.

I vividly remember the stand-up rehearsals. Jim had them videotaped, and he paraded around like the director on a movie set. "Stop the video," he'd shout. "You have to lay out the story with enthusiasm!" Then, for the umpteenth time, he'd order us to start over. More than once, he rearranged the 25-minute presentation to make Sean and Tom's roles more prominent. My part was that of the senior executive directing the company's young executives to implement the business plan.

We started each presentation with a list of selling points designed to attract investors. We showcased ourselves as **specialists, mixed marketers, product innovators, and underwriters with growth potential and a national footprint.**

The actual road show itself was grueling. Starting in August, we crisscrossed the country from Boston to San Francisco, landing in all the major cities in between. Then we headed to London to visit Warburg's office there. All told, we were on the road for two and a half weeks, keeping six to eight appointments a day. Despite the stress and fatigue, we loved every minute. Once we settled in to the routine, we relaxed and started to have fun. After each day we tried to assess who liked our story and who placed the largest order. One morning while presenting in Chicago, the analyst seemed totally disconnected – eating a doughnut and drinking coffee. We were all sure he wasn't a buyer. Turns out, he put in the high order of the day. Sean remembers that the Sultan of Brunei was staying at our hotel in London. "We thought it was funny that a little

2,800,000 Shares

Philadelphia Consolidated Holding Corp.

Philadelphia Insurance Companies

Common Stock

||||

All shares of Common Stock offered hereby are being sold by Philadelphia Consolidated Holding Corp., doing business as "Philadelphia Insurance Companies" ("Philadelphia Insurance").

Prior to this offering, there has been no public market for the Common Stock of Philadelphia Insurance. See "Underwriting" for information relating to the determination of the initial public offering price. The Common Stock has been approved for quotation on the NASDAQ National Market System under the symbol "PHLY."

AN INVESTMENT IN THE SHARES OF COMMON STOCK OFFERED HEREBY INVOLVES A SUBSTANTIAL DEGREE OF RISK. SEE "INVESTMENT CONSIDERATIONS."

THESE SECURITIES HAVE NOT BEEN APPROVED OR DISAPPROVED BY THE SECURITIES AND EXCHANGE COMMISSION OR ANY STATE SECURITIES COMMISSION NOR HAS THE SECURITIES AND EXCHANGE COMMISSION OR ANY STATE SECURITIES COMMISSION PASSED UPON THE ACCURACY OR ADEQUACY OF THIS PROSPECTUS. ANY REPRESENTATION TO THE CONTRARY IS A CRIMINAL OFFENSE.

	Price to Public	Underwriting Discount[1]	Proceeds to Company[2]
Per Share	$13.00	$0.91	$12.09
Total[3]	$36,400,000	$2,548,000	$33,852,000

(1) *Philadelphia Insurance has agreed to indemnify the Underwriters against certain liabilities, including liabilities under the Securities Act of 1933. See "Underwriting."*

(2) *Before deducting expenses payable by Philadelphia Insurance, estimated at $500,000.*

(3) *Philadelphia Insurance has granted the several Underwriters a 30-day option to purchase up to an additional 420,000 shares of Common Stock to cover over-allotments, if any. If all such shares are purchased, the total Price to Public, Underwriting Discount and Proceeds to Company will be $41,860,000, $2,930,200, and $38,929,800 respectively. See "Underwriting."*

The shares of Common Stock are offered by the several Underwriters, subject to prior sale, when, as and if issued to and accepted by the Underwriters, subject to approval of certain legal matters by counsel for the Underwriters. The Underwriters reserve the right to withdraw, cancel or modify such offer and reject orders in whole or in part. It is expected that delivery of the shares of Common Stock will be made in New York, New York on or about September 23, 1993.

S.G. Warburg & Co. Inc.   The Chicago Corporation

▸ IPO

September, 1993

▶ Tony Ursano
Chaperoned our first road show

company like ours was rubbing elbows with one of the world's richest men," he says, "but we also thought we were very cool!"

Our point man during the road show was Tony Ursano, a recent graduate of the University of North Carolina, whom Jim Zech had hired at Warburg. Tony scheduled our presentations, made arrangements for our lodging, meals, and travel, and generally saw to it that everything ran smoothly. Tony had been a star lacrosse player for the Tar Heels and packed about 225 pounds on his six-foot-two-inch frame. Even at his young age, Tony had a presence, and he knew how to keep us pumped and ready to go at each increasingly exhausting stop. Five years after our IPO we would ask Tony, now at Merrill Lynch, to work with us again when we returned to Wall Street for more capital.

PHLY had gone from $1.58 to $61.50 per share. A 3,800 percent return for original investors.

Investors were clearly attracted by my 33 years of experience, but the ability to present two poised, knowledgeable, energetic, and confident senior officers was a strong selling point. Both Sean and Tom had complete command of company facts and figures. They so thoroughly understood our business plan and products that I often deferred to them when our audiences had questions. Sean's energy in particular drew attention. At a luncheon in New York, one audience member said ours was the most enthusiastic IPO presentation he'd ever witnessed, at which point Sean piped up to say, "This is probably the best insurance company you've ever seen also!" At lunch that day Larry Ariani, CEO of the Kaufman Fund, told me he was buying 300,000 shares.

Years later when we consummated our merger with Tokio Marine, Larry called and congratulated me. He told me he'd increased his position to over one million shares and said Warren Buffett's growth paled in comparison to the 28 percent compound annual growth of PHLY. On a split adjusted basis, PHLY had gone from $1.58 to $61.50 per share. A 3,800 percent return for original investors.

The Maguire Insurance Agency was and is our marketing company, fully licensed in all states and able to broker any part of an account we didn't want to underwrite. While on the road show I repeatedly said "there are two things my company and I will never do: We don't write workers' comp and I don't cheat on my wife." Since most business accounts want workers' comp, we brokered that part of the account to either a state fund or a company that insured such business. The message was simple: no long-tail business and integrity from the top down.

Discipline plus execution was our formula for success.

Aware that our 20-office marketing network could be seen as a weakness for a company looking to claim national status, we presented it to investors as a pressing concern we would remedy with the offering proceeds. We turned a negative into a positive by preemptively identifying the 30 major U.S. markets we didn't serve and outlining our plans to enter those markets.

Buoyed by the investor community interest, none of us ever had a moment's doubt about completing the offering. The IPO was oversubscribed by 300 percent.

On September 16, 1993, the Philadelphia Insurance Companies sold 3,220,000 of its shares – including the so-called "green-shoe" allotment of 420,000 shares that went to the underwriting syndicate to cover unexpected demand – for a total of $41.9 million. Teaser sheets that had been prepared and distributed by the bankers before and during the road show gave a price range between $11.50 and $13.50 a share. On the day of the sale, Warburg's pricing desk set the price at $13.

Prior to the offering, I insisted that all of our key people receive a 25,000 share stock option at the offering price, with a five-year cliff vesting, meaning that the benefits would accrue to the employees after five years rather than gradually over the course of five years. I thought it was important to reward them for helping us get this far, while also locking them in for the next phase of our growth.

Winning the State Championship

Sean, Tom, and I spent the afternoon of September 17, settlement day, in Warburg's New York offices. The oversubscription meant that our road-show investors would get fewer shares than most had ordered, and some orders would not be filled at all, which made for a stronger aftermarket.

At the end of one of the most important days of my life, I headed home to Frannie in Philadelphia. We were like two kids whose high school team had just won the state championship. We had gone from a 400-square-foot walk-up office over a bakery to a publicly traded company with the symbol PHLY on the NASDAQ stock exchange.

We had gone from a 400-square-foot walk-up office over a bakery to a publicly traded company ....

▸ **PHLY goes Public 1993**

The next morning dawned bright and beautiful, and Frannie and I enjoyed breakfast on our patio. Our feeling of achievement and pride was overwhelming. It was a moment to savor.

Craig Keller met me when I arrived at the office and couldn't stop smiling when he told me that $41.9 million had just been wired into our account. Giddy is the only word to describe how Sean, Tom, Craig, and I felt as congratulatory phone calls poured into the office from around the country.

But with our euphoria came a new sense of purpose. We had raised $41.9 million to write the next chapters of our story, and we were determined not to let our investors down. That afternoon, I had a conference call with our regional managers. I reminded them that Wall Street had shown great confidence in the PHLY story. I could feel the excitement that day, a euphoria like a Notre Dame team after a Lou Holtz halftime pep talk.

With the proceeds from the IPO, we paid off the remainder of the mezzanine financing and the debt incurred in buying back the warrants. We were debt-free with a statutory policyholder surplus of $42.2 million. What's more, our newly expanded capital position gave us the ability to secure insurance company licenses in the remaining 16 states, which would bring us to 50.

The Afterglow of a Triumph

On October 11, 1993, Warburg and the Chicago Corporation hosted a celebratory dinner at the Four Seasons Hotel in Philadelphia. After thanking everyone who helped to make the IPO a success, I unveiled my five-year plan and shared my vision of our future. Convinced that we could dominate the specialty niche business within a decade, I said that I planned to use our IPO money to develop a cutting-edge systems capability, new products, build a management team for the 21st century, and beef up our marketing capabilities by fulfilling my road-show promise to open new locations and add field representatives nationwide.

10-in-1: Joins 10 Reasons Why

The key to our future success, as it had been in the past, would be our ability to attract and train high achievers to select and underwrite good business. I also introduced the next innovation of our marketing strategy: The 10-in-1 Plan. Instead of concentrating on direct sales, our field representatives were directed to build a relationship with 10 independent brokers who were familiar with one or more of our niche products. "We will find out who our 10 best competitors are in each territory, and get them to do business with us."

"The insured makes the buying decision" had long been our mantra. But, often, customers attracted by one or more of our niche products wanted their own brokers to be involved. In the case of social-services accounts, for example, some brokers actually sat on the nonprofits' boards. We were willing to present our product to a customer's broker, but we wanted our enhanced coverage – "the 10 reasons why" – included with the quote.

The brokers would write more business because our marketing people worked with them to unearth new accounts, while also supplying them with a superior product.

In mid-1995, Sean Sweeney took the 10-in-1 Plan one step further by introducing the preferred agent program. It recognized and rewarded loyal brokers who consistently placed niche business with PHLY. Underwriting success was always our goal, so it made sense to financially reward those agents who helped us reach our underwriting targets.

To become a preferred agent, a broker had to give us the right of first refusal on business that fit our niche. We, in turn, promised to funnel leads to him. The real advantage of the preferred agent program came down to this: We created a business partnership where both sides were winners.

Joining forces with the broker community would prove to be one of the best marketing decisions we ever made.

Our preferred-agent agreements won unexpected affirmation in 2004 when former New York Attorney General Eliot Spitzer sued the big insurance brokerage houses, alleging a pay-to-play scheme. Spitzer charged that the brokerages steered large volumes of business to companies promising larger commissions. Philadelphia Insurance's profit-share agreements were subpoenaed by the attorney general and held up under his scrutiny. Our preferred agents, some of whom had groused about having to wait for bonuses until profits could be determined, were glad to receive a share of actual profits rather than a kickback for creating volume.

By June 1996, when we hosted our first conference in Philadelphia, 35 agents had earned preferred status. Today, there are almost 300 preferred agents, an agent advisory board, and over 800 Firemark agents (agents working to gain preferred status).

The Tigers Begin to Roar

While I was putting the pieces in place to go public, my youngest son, Tim, received his B.S. degree from Saint Joseph's University on May 19, 1993. There was a celebration at the company and in the Maguire house.

Tim had come to work for us right out of high school and after two years in college opted to finish his degree studies at night school. Despite being the son of the CEO, Tim came on as an entry-level employee and received no special treatment. He spent his first summer in the mailroom before moving to the claims department and then into a sales-training program. While earning his degree, he was learning to become a professional in the insurance industry. So when Tim graduated and we found ourselves with a vacant sales position in the Southern California office, I asked him to fill it. Thus began another incredible success story at PHLY that served to augment the double-digit growth of our company.

In his first 36 months in California, Tim's transformation in the San Juan Capistrano office was nothing short of spectacular. At year-end 1996, he reported $3.6 million of in-force

▶ **Tim graduates from Saint Joseph's University 1993**
Jim and Frannie, Tim, Megan, and Franny. He left for Southern California to fill a vacant sales position. Thus began an incredible success story.

▶ **Tim Maguire - Senior Vice President**
In recognition of his accomplishments, he was promoted to senior vice president in 2005.

business with a profitable cumulative loss ratio, and a staff he expanded from two people to a full complement of 12 professionals. Philadelphia Insurance was becoming a Southern California force to be reckoned with.

When Tim moved the operation to new and larger quarters in 1998, I attended the ribbon-cutting ceremony and open house that drew 150 agents. I'll long remember with great pride the praise they heaped on Tim that day. In recognition of his accomplishments, I elevated him that year to

An athlete in the Maguire mold

Tim completed a dozen Ironman competitions including two Hawaii Ironman races.

regional vice president of the company's Sun Belt operations.

Fast-forward to 2005, when we split the country into three territories: Bob O'Leary was tapped to manage the East, Bob Pottle was given the Midwest, and Tim was chosen to manage the Western territory, comprising 16 offices in 13 states with 200 employees and a half-billion dollars of in-force business. What is so impressive about Tim is the humble and low-key way in which he went about achieving his remarkable success.

An athlete in the Maguire mold, Tim was the first among us to complete an Ironman competition and followed up with 12 more, including two Hawaii Ironman races and one 56-mile ultramarathon. The fitness culture he spawned became infectious, and he took it to a whole new level by sponsoring the Challenged Athlete Foundation Pacific Coast Triathlon, where he now serves on the board. Tim has raised awareness of disabled athletes and the day-to-day challenges they face, including American soldiers injured in the line of duty who must rebuild their lives upon returning home.

Tim is quick to say that the success of the Western territory is shared by his four regional vice presidents – Bryan Luci, Chuck Pedone, Ken Klassy, and Shannon Weston. "They are loyal,

Ken Klassy
Regional Vice President Northwest

dedicated high achievers who made the Western territory the success it is."

As a public company, our formula for success remained unchanged. We'd find young talent, articulate and define our culture, train them, and give them an opportunity to succeed. Over the years, we had no lack of young talent capable of assuming leadership roles.

Ken Klassy opened our first Northwest office, in Portland, Oregon, and later added Seattle and Boise, Idaho. From a dead start in 1990 he's built an organization of 27 employees, which in 2009 recorded $100 million of written premium.

Craig Keller had stepped in to run the accounting department in 1992 after Bob Wilkin suffered a heart attack and decided to retire. Craig also took on the responsibility of building a complete financial division with a staff capable of handling internal audits, monthly reporting, annual updates of our five-year business plan, and tax matters. In the years immediately following the IPO, when faced with rigorous reporting deadlines, Craig stayed cool.

▸ **Craig Keller**
When Wall Street reporting deadlines were bedeviling us,
Craig stayed cool.

My son Chris, who was moving up in the underwriting department, had become fully aware of the link between successful underwriting and profitability. A vocal advocate for treating sales and underwriting talent equally, Chris opened my eyes. The salesman in me had long been focused on bringing in business. Underwriting and pricing were important, I knew, but it was the salespeople who were given incentives to excel.

Chris started a movement for change in 1994 by initiating underwriting responsibilities for our marketing organization. No longer would we issue quotes to any and all comers. Chris laid out a set of non-negotiable underwriting standards that, in effect, made marketing the first line of defense against unprofitable accounts. From that time on, every application sent to the home office, among other things, had to include a three-year loss history from the previous carrier.

The new standards dramatically improved our quotes to sold accounts. When we encountered a broker with a book of business that he wanted to roll over to us, we would underwrite each account, rejecting the unprofitable ones. **We didn't subscribe to the notion that you had to take the bad with the good.**

▸ **Chris joins company - January 1987**
and changed the sales culture to underwriting.

With Tim in sales and Chris in underwriting, an interesting dynamic developed. Tim was eager to sell an account and Chris was intent on measuring exposure and pricing it adequately. What might have been clashing objectives started coming together in the best interests of the company. There were tense moments, of course, but the culture of our family business encouraged compromise and taught empathy.

Chris started a movement for change in 1994 by initiating underwriting responsibilities for our marketing organization.

Product Development Comes of Age

Nineteen ninety-four was a watershed year for the product development committee. I had long viewed it as crucial to our future growth, and it was both exciting and gratifying to see it finally come into its own.

As I have said throughout my career, even unique products have a shelf life. We knew when it was time to retire WHEELWAYS, as difficult as that was for some people to accept. No matter how popular your program is, it will eventually lose altitude. You can fly only so high before competitors launch missiles to bring you down or steal some of your market share. Their warheads may contain lower pricing, risky special coverage, or some other wrinkle. When this happens, you must have new products on the drawing board.

In organizing our product-development committee, we included representatives from all the company disciplines; an employee working in any corner of the company might run across a complaint, request, or unforeseen situation that could spark a new product idea. We also drafted our preferred agents into the new-product army and aggressively solicited their ideas. From their vantage points in hundreds of communities nationwide, they gave us insight into what the customer wanted and what competitors were offering.

When evaluating a new product idea, our development committee researched the insurance service office (ISO) database for information about risk. A new offering also had to meet established criteria concerning critical mass, return on investment, market competition, expected penetration, ultimate combined ratio, and price sensitivity. For any new idea that passed muster, reinsurance support had to be arranged and filings made. And, finally, before the trigger was pulled, a new program had to be incubated in a test program for up to a year.

One of our new-product niches in the 1990s was the outdoor recreation business. There were few competitors, a broad geographic spread, premiums too small to catch the attention of large brokers, and an actuarial history of profit. But the piece that made this niche a natural for us was its need for uniquely tailored coverage. Our main competitor was Colorado-based Gillingham & Associates, with whom we had competed for many years before eventually buying the company in 2008.

Each month, our products were reviewed with the intent of adding cutting-edge enhancements, any one of which could end up on the list of "10 Reasons Why." That's what happened when we upgraded our health and fitness coverage by adding subcontractor liability for fitness trainers. With few or no other options, trainers began doing our sales work for us, recommending Philadelphia Insurance to the owners of the facilities where they worked. Today, our fitness trainer's liability insurance covers over 18,000 fitness trainers.

As 1995 drew to a close, the nonprofit social-service business was our largest niche product, representing 25 percent of our business. The company had grown to $104.2 million of gross written premium, with $9.8 million of net income. Thanks to the marketing department underwriting initiative started by Chris, our combined ratio was 86.5 percent, roughly 15 percent better than the industry average.

Best of all: I had a core group of loyal, smart, and dedicated people who would help me build an enduring company.

Philadelphia Insurance Companies Financial Results 1991–1995

(In Thousands)

	1991	1992	1993	1994	1995
▸ GAAP Gross Written Premium	$ 26,341	$ 37,202	$ 57,085	$ 89,099	$ 104,180
▸ GAAP Net Income (Loss)	$ (1)	$ 944	$ 4,232	$ 5,973	$ 9,830
▸ GAAP Combined Ratio	94.9%	96.3%	91.1%	89.4%	86.5%
▸ Statutory Combined Ratio	92.8%	95.8%	91.0%	89.4%	86.7%

"Traits of a leader:

Selflessness, Commitment, Perseverance"

James J. Maguire
Founder, Philadelphia Insurance Companies

Chapter 14

A Dream Fulfilled

▶ **1996 Annual Report**

The cover of our 1996 annual report pictured Philadelphia City Hall with William Penn atop, set against the backdrop of the city's newest skyscraper, Liberty Place. Our intent was to suggest a parallel between the stability and growth of the city with that of our company. Inside the cover were financial results proving that growth was indeed a hallmark of the company. In the three years since our IPO, revenue had increased by 100 percent and earnings by 300 percent. In addition, A.M. Best had elevated our rating to A (excellent) in May 1996, which freed us to eliminate many of the costly fronting fees we had been forced to pay after losing our rating. Now, we could do business as we saw fit.

Our nonprofit program, now in its seventh year, had gained such credibility with social service agencies that legions of them were now clients. In another major niche, big fitness chains such as Gold's Gym, Total Fitness, and Leisure Sports were now our clients. And where the big gyms went, the smaller independants followed.

With business growing so rapidly, we had no trouble attracting talented and motivated people. We were assembling a team that would enable us to achieve our goal of becoming the best niche insurance company in the United States. And in the process, I hoped the line of succession at the top of the company would become clear.

▸ 1996 - Jamie returns to PHLY

The Prodigal Son Returns

My oldest son, Jamie, was now an AIG assistant vice president with considerable experience as a professional liability underwriter. He was living less than two hours away in Summit, New Jersey, and we had discussed his career many times, always with the possibility that he might one day rejoin the family business. In the years since Jamie left Philadelphia much had changed, including me.

I had come late to the realization that my son was his own man and didn't need me to dictate or approve his every move. With my newfound understanding, I felt some regret for having managed my family as if it were a business. Rules, regimentation, and a dependence on metrics may boost a company's performance, but a family raised by a drill sergeant is a family short on love. I most certainly loved my family; in retrospect, I may not have shown it enough when the children were growing up.

Rules, regimentation, and a dependence on metrics may boost a company's performance, but a family raised by a drill sergeant is a family short on love.

However, as a father I always felt my primary responsibility was to build character, which required me to be a disciplinarian. Thank God for Frannie, who made up for all the love I didn't show.

In late April 1996, Frannie and I went to visit Jamie and Lisa in Summit. PHLY had just released first-quarter results showing 27 percent year-over-year growth in earnings and a 24 percent increase in shareholders' equity. Our stock was trading at $22 per share, up from $13, facts which Jamie knew well. We talked at length about his position at AIG, and without warning I blurted out, "Come back to Philadelphia!" I had clearly taken him by surprise, and saying I wanted him back riveted his attention. I could sense that he was excited at the thought of returning.

> *Thank God for Frannie, who made up for all the love I didn't show.*

Jamie made me a very happy man the following month when he agreed to return to the company. After several weeks of negotiating, he came back as a vice president responsible for establishing a professional liability division. This was his area of expertise, and I acknowledged that fact by acceding to his request for stock options, a moving allowance, performance bonus, employment contract, and leadership role in which he would be reporting directly to me.

▸ **Tom Nerney**
He was a born leader.

I hired my son without consulting anyone else, given that he would be responsible to no one but me. I made a point of introducing him as a highly qualified executive with just the kind of talent we needed. Craig Keller and Sean, always team players, eagerly welcomed Jamie back. Chris, who had been assuming more and more responsibility in the underwriting department, and who had clearly taken a leadership position, was also excited about his brother's return. Not so Tom Nerney.

Anticipating Jamie's return, and wanting Tom to understand that he was a key part of our company, I had recently promoted him to chief operating officer. However, Tom was upset at having been excluded from the hiring process. He was also uneasy about Jamie reporting directly to me – he felt he should have some oversight of Jamie's work. More to the point, Tom thought I was anointing Jamie as the heir apparent and quashing his chances of ever becoming CEO.

Tom was like a son to me, but he clearly viewed Jamie as a new and insurmountable obstacle blocking his path to the top job. If Jamie came back to the company with a grand plan to seize the reins, it was never discussed and I never saw it. I truly believed that as a growing company there was plenty of room for talent. In any event, I didn't expect to be replaced anytime soon. At 62, I thought I had at least 13 more good years before I'd need to name a successor, and I expected to choose between a number of first-rate candidates – Tom, Jamie, Sean, Chris, Bob O'Leary, and others.

▸ 1997 - *Forbes* names PHLY number 71 of the 200 Best Small Companies.

Two days after I announced Jamie's return, Tom requested a leave of absence to think about the direction of his career. Two weeks later, he returned to work and announced his resignation. Did he have any other job prospects, I asked. He admitted that he did not. I was devastated to see him go. Over the past 18 years, he had become like a son to me; his wife, Jill, and their family were a part of our family.

As much as I hated to lose this bright young man, I knew he was on solid financial footing. The value of his stock options was substantial; he could afford to take his time finding the right position.

About a month later, a headhunter called with a list of questions about Tom: Why did he leave? Was he qualified to run an insurance company? Would I rehire him? What had been his compensation? Was he honest, ethical, and hardworking? I answered "yes," or a positive equivalent, to every question.

I spent at least 35 minutes talking about Tom, emphasizing that he would make a great CEO. When the headhunter identified his client as the United States Liability Insurance Company – which Warren Buffett would eventually purchase through his Berkshire Hathaway holding company – I said Tom was the perfect choice. Tom landed the job and in short order turned what was a sleepy company into a competitive player.

Jamie Shows His Mettle

Jamie made his presence felt almost immediately. He drafted our Executive Safeguard proprietary package policy, which included Directors and Officers, employment-practices, fiduciary-liability, and kidnap and ransom coverage for both public and private companies. The package was an immediate success, helping lead the way to huge gains in the specialty-lines division. Indeed, two and a half years after Jamie's return, the division could boast a 100 percent gain in gross revenue, while the bottom line showed a 30 percent profit margin on the strength of new product introductions and better performance within the division overall.

Joined PHLY in 1988

▸ **Ted Brogan, VP, Harrisburg, PA**
Middle Atlantic States

In 1997, we were happy to be recognized by *Forbes* magazine as one of the "200 Best Small Companies in America." The criteria used to judge the recipients of the annual award are consistent growth, profitability, return on equity, and combined ratio – our ratio was 85.9 percent, again outperforming the industry by 16 points. Only four insurance companies made the list of 200 that year.

Joined PHLY in 1990

After four years as a public company, thanks to the expansion efforts headed by Sean Sweeney, we had 17 new offices and 100 new employees. Our top-line growth exceeded 150 percent and annual profits grew 42 percent.

The Princeton, New Jersey, office that opened in 1995 is typical of how we built our national presence, and Brian O'Reilly epitomizes the PHLY success story. Brian came to the company in 1990 right out of Lafayette College, where he was an academic high achiever and star soccer player. He was trained in sales by Ted

▸ **Brian O'Reilly, Regional Vice President**
Metro Region

▶ **William Benecke, Executive Vice President
Director of Claims**

Brogan over the course of four years, before receiving the assignment to open a new office in Princeton, NJ. In 2004, Brian was promoted to regional vice president and by 2009 the region had 75 employees, with $275 million of business under management.

This "new office business model" developed by Sean Sweeney was repeated successfully throughout the country.

As successful as we were in developing a strong marketing presence, insurance companies are only as good as their claims service. Bill Benecke, who joined the company in the summer of 1990, came to us with five years of industry claims experience at Ohio Casualty. He had been with us for two years when it came to my attention that our claims manager was leaving at 2:00 P.M. every day to play golf. Much as I love sports, a golf junkie managing my claims department was not part of my plan, so I fired him and put Bill in charge.

Bill was subsequently promoted up the ladder to executive vice president in 2006. He has won praise for seeking out and implementing the technology needed to make the claims department a highly efficient, paperless operation with claims service in our regional offices throughout the country.

**Company receives A+ (superior)
Rating in 1998**

▶ **Financial Strength - AM Best**

Another Cash Infusion from Wall Street

The best time to raise money is when Wall Street is hungry for new offerings – and before you begin to feel the need for more capital. The year 1998 was just such a time. We had 53 preferred agents in a growing program that was producing excellent results, while our niche products – particularly professional liability and the still-expanding social-service program – worked like magnets to bring in new customers. We were like a basketball team with momentum; everyone from the rookies to our seasoned professionals were making their shots.

Using Sean's Sales-Trac processing system, we logged every contact for follow-up and recorded every quotation for future reference. The system also allowed every office to monitor and recall its accounts, thus enabling accurate assessments of future growth. At the same time, Chris was busy developing the P.A.T.H. (PHLY Access To Home office) reservation system to track and image the underwriting work flow.

With detailed information at our fingertips, our business plan projected that growth over the coming four years would match the 20 percent posted in each of the past four. Raising money now would give us the capital to support our projected growth by adding preferred agents and new staff. Furthermore, we had our eye on an acquisition opportunity, Liberty American Insurance Company, a Tampa, Florida-based company that Chris had done business with as a preferred agent.

In April, we contacted Tony Ursano, our IPO road show coordinator, who had left Jim Zech and Warburg to become the managing director of insurance mergers and acquisitions at Merrill Lynch. Eager to do a deal in his new capacity, Tony put together a very attractive $103.5 million three-year, 7 percent preferred convertible offering.

We were like a basketball team with momentum ...

The only tense moment came during the negotiations when Tony wanted me to cover half the cost of the private jet that would be flying us around the country. He said it was standard practice for the client to split the bill with Merrill. When I refused, Tony dug in, declaring that Merrill would not go forward with the offering unless I ponied up.

"I guess we don't have a deal, then," I replied. Clearly taken aback, Tony said, "You mean to tell me you'd walk away from a $100 million deal over $30,000?" Tony very nearly lost his composure, but I knew he was too smart to let the deal sour. Merrill paid for the plane.

The road show, which was oversubscribed, lasted just one week. Investors saw our track record of growth and profit and many of our existing stockholders brought up the offering. It was the perfect opportunity to showcase Jamie and Sean as the next generation of PHLY leaders.

9,000,000 FELINE PRIDES^{SM}

(Consisting of 8,000,000 Income PRIDES^{SM} and 1,000,000 Growth PRIDES^{SM})

PHILADELPHIA CONSOLIDATED HOLDING CORP.

Philadelphia Insurance Companies

1,000,000 Trust Preferred Securities^{SM}
PCHC Financing I
7% Trust Originated Preferred Securities^{SM} ("TOPrS"^{SM})
(Liquidation Amount $10 per Trust Preferred Security)
fully and unconditionally guaranteed to
the extent set forth herein by
Philadelphia Consolidated Holding Corp.

The securities offered hereby are 9,000,000 FELINE PRIDES^{SM} ("FELINE PRIDES") of Philadelphia Consolidated Holding Corp., a Pennsylvania corporation ("Philadelphia Consolidated" or the "Company"), and 1,000,000 7.00% Trust Originated Preferred Securities (the "Trust Preferred Securities" and, together with the FELINE PRIDES, the "Securities") of PCHC Financing I, a statutory business trust formed under the laws of the State of Delaware (the "Trust"), having a stated liquidation amount per Trust Preferred Security equal to $10. Initially, 8,000,000 Trust Preferred Securities will be issued and held as a component of

(continued on next page)

See "Risk Factors" beginning on Page S-26 of this Prospectus Supplement for certain information relevant to an investment in the Securities.

Prior to the offering made hereby there has been no public market for the Securities. The Income PRIDES and the Growth PRIDES have been approved for listing on the Nasdaq National Market (the "NNM") of The Nasdaq Stock Market Inc. under the symbols "PHLYZ" and "PHLYL", subject to official notice of issuance. If the Trust Preferred Securities are separately traded to a sufficient extent that the applicable market listing requirements are met, the Company will endeavor to cause such securities to be listed on the market on which the Income PRIDES and the Growth PRIDES are then listed including, if applicable, the NNM. On April 28, 1998, the last reported sale price of the Common Stock on the NNM was $21¼ per share.

THESE SECURITIES HAVE NOT BEEN APPROVED OR DISAPPROVED BY THE SECURITIES AND EXCHANGE COMMISSION OR ANY STATE SECURITIES COMMISSION, NOR HAS THE SECURITIES AND EXCHANGE COMMISSION OR ANY STATE SECURITIES COMMISSION PASSED UPON THE ACCURACY OR ADEQUACY OF THIS PROSPECTUS SUPPLEMENT OR THE PROSPECTUS TO WHICH IT RELATES. ANY REPRESENTATION TO THE CONTRARY IS A CRIMINAL OFFENSE.

Price to Public(1)
$10.000 per Income PRIDES
$8.501 per Growth PRIDES
$9.933 per Trust Preferred Security

	Underwriting Commission(2)	Proceeds to Company(3)
Total(4)	$2,925,000	$87,075,000

(1) Plus, as applicable, accrued distributions, interest and Contract Adjustment Payments, if any, from May 4, 1998. The purchase price of each Income PRIDES and Growth PRIDES will be allocated between the related Purchase Contract and the related Trust Preferred Security, in the case of Income PRIDES, and interest in a Treasury Security, in the case of Growth PRIDES, as applicable, in proportion to their respective fair market values at the time of purchase. See "Certain Federal Income Tax Consequences — FELINE PRIDES — Allocation of Purchase Price."

(2) Philadelphia Consolidated and the Trust have agreed to indemnify the Underwriters against certain liabilities under the Securities Act of 1933, as amended. See "Underwriting."

(3) Before deducting expenses payable by Philadelphia Consolidated estimated at $516,000; such amount does not include $8,433,900 used to purchase the Treasury Securities component of the 1,000,000 Growth PRIDES.

(4) Philadelphia Consolidated and the Trust have granted to the Underwriters 30-day options to purchase up to an additional 1,200,000 Income PRIDES, 150,000 Growth PRIDES and 150,000 Trust Preferred Securities, to cover over-allotments, if any; provided, however, that the Underwriters must purchase at least as many Trust Preferred Securities as Growth PRIDES. If such options are exercised in full, the total Underwriting Commission and Proceeds to Philadelphia Consolidated will be $3,363,750 and $100,136,250 (such amount does not include approximately $9,698,985 used to purchase the Treasury Securities component of the Growth PRIDES), respectively. See "Underwriting."

Merrill Lynch & Co.

CIBC Oppenheimer

Schroder & Co. Inc.

The date of this Prospectus Supplement is April 28, 1998.

▸ Company raises $103,500,000 of new capital; 3 year, 7% coupon, preferred convertible stock

Embarrassed by the Jelly-Doughnut Gang

Later that year, we began a specialty property and inland marine division that turned out to be about as stinky as a three-day-old fish. General Accident Insurance Company, a longtime fixture in Philadelphia, was bought by Commercial Union Assurance Company, Ltd. and relocated to Boston. Eight employees in the company's specialty property division, including its vice president, didn't want to leave the Philadelphia area. Thinking their unique expertise in large-property and inland-marine risks would give us a competitive advantage, we hired the eight division holdouts as well as six of their salespeople located around the country.

Six months into the arrangement, red flags began to fly. We were receiving claims from customers we had no record of billing. I sent Sean to the property department to find out what was going on. What he discovered was a department completely devoid of the PHLY culture: our passion for strict procedure was missing. There was no underwriting and pricing control.

After nine months of unfathomably sloppy performance on the part of our erstwhile colleagues, we pulled the plug on what Sean called the "jelly-doughnut gang." The division employees who did bother to show up in the morning usually began their day around a conference table loaded with jelly doughnuts.

Months of culture shock on both sides of the divide ended with every last one of this hapless crew being fired. Undeterred by our doughnut escapade, we re-staffed the division and went on to develop a successful large property niche.

Forbes again honored us for our accomplishments by naming us to its 1999 list of America's Best 200 Small Companies, our second consecutive award.

Succession on My Mind

I had begun thinking about succession before the 1998 road show. I knew I was fortunate to have three strong candidates – Jamie, Sean, and Chris – all of whom were highly qualified. Before our third-quarter board meeting, I discussed my feelings with Eustace Wolfington, Paul Hertel, Mike Morris, and Roger Larson. Chris drew praise for his underwriting smarts and work ethic, but they felt that Jamie and Sean were the top contenders for the job of president and, ultimately, CEO. Eustace, who had spent his entire career in marketing, expressed his opinion that taking Sean out of marketing would be a mistake for the company.

Several companies had been wooing Sean with a CEO position. I would never want to risk losing Sean, but was sure he wouldn't leave us for several reasons: First, he was totally loyal to me and the company. He had played a major role in our success, and, second, he was no dummy. Sean already held stock options worth substantially more than anything his suitors could offer.

In October 1998, I took the first step in the succession plan by promoting Jamie to executive vice president and chief operating officer, Sean to executive vice president and director of field operations, and Chris to senior vice president and chief underwriting officer. With these promotions and the capital infusion, the company was positioned to continue its profitable growth in the 21st century.

Joined PHLY in 1983

▶ **P. Daniel Eldridge, CPCU, President and Chief Executive Officer**
Liberty American Insurance Group

In July 1999, we acquired Liberty American, paying $45 million for an entity that produced $81 million of annual premium. What drew us to the company was its expertise in homeowners and manufactured housing, in addition to its network of agents. Initially, we planned to expand its personal lines business beyond Florida and Arizona to 13 additional states.

The first year was frustrating. Growth was sluggish, and the company's leaders had lost their drive after receiving the payout. I flew to Tampa, bid farewell to the two brothers running the company, and summoned Dan Eldridge, our regional vice president in Orlando. Dan pulled up stakes and moved to Tampa to spearhead a turnaround. For the next four years, he successfully ran Liberty American.

Dan, who had joined PHLY in 1983, was originally hired as a marketing representative. He was competitive, smart, organized, and loyal. A six-foot, two-inch scholarship basketball player from the University of Tennessee at Chattanooga, Dan was handsome, soft-spoken, and displayed the attitude of a winner.

In 1988, he was promoted to regional vice president of our Southeastern territory and over the next 10 years under his supervision, the territory grew a staggering 1,000 percent, posting $100 million in revenue.

Managing Liberty America

We had always been purchasers of reinsurance. On large property exposures, it was our practice to retain the first $1 million of loss (later increased to $10 million) and then purchase excess coverage (reinsurance) up to the value of the property. We did the same for Florida, a potential disaster area, buying reinsurance based on certain actuarial formulas.

In 2004, when Florida was battered by a series of four hurricanes over a span of 40 days, Liberty American found itself facing $660 million of gross property losses. Fortunately, Chris, in his role as chief underwriting officer, had purchased $750 million of catastrophe reinsurance in excess of a $10 million loss retention. That treaty also included additional reinsurance to provide automatic reinstatement of coverage after a loss. In the end, with four hurricanes in 40 days, we paid $10 million per event, or a total of $40 million, and $620 million was submitted to and recovered from our reinsurers, thus leaving our capital intact.

It was in 2004 that Chris and Dan first met Tokio Marine in Bermuda, when they subscribed to part of our Florida reinsurance treaty. (Little did we know that one day we would be acquired by them.)

Jamie Articulates His Vision

At the October 1999 board meeting, I took the next step in the succession plan by naming Jamie president. I was very proud when he accepted the promotion and briefly articulated his vision for the company.

"To have top-line premium growth without favorable underwriting results is not an option," Jamie declared. In addition, "employees should be able to get work-related information anywhere at any time and that requires us to improve our technology. It means leading the company away

Joined PHLY in 1992

from its legacy information system to a Web-based client data system that is scalable as the company grows." Finally, Jamie promised to be the "champion of culture perpetuation," which he called the "key to our success."

When I look back at the progress – going from a legacy mainframe to a client-server and then a Web-based system, from paper underwriting manuals to a collaborative online shared directory and a corporate intranet, the enormity of our progress is impressive. What made it all work was the operating process put in place to use these systems.

▶ **Debbie Sutton, Director of Human Resources**

We established objectives for every discipline and had measures in place to assure constant work flow. If rating, quoting, or issuing hit a snag or bogged down, we could identify where and why it happened and fix it. Management by objective was being used in real time.

As the year 1999 rolled over to 2000 without the cataclysmic crash of the world's computers so loudly predicted by the Y2K doomsayers, we found a silver lining in the hysteria. Besides making the computer fixes designed to avert Armageddon, we took the opportunity to standardize all of our database management applications. In addition, we upgraded all of our office systems around the country so that employees could submit new accounts to the home office and access claim records and accounts receivable information online in real time.

The year 2000 also saw the creation of a true Human Resources department. Debbie Sutton, who had been overseeing the department from her post in operations, was given formal responsibility in 2001, when we named her senior vice president of human resources and operations. In keeping with our culture of teamwork and individual excellence, Jamie was determined to have Philadelphia Insurance be recognized as one of the best companies to work for in the United States. We introduced a number of new benefits, such as flextime, a larger 401(k) matching contribution, and expanded health coverage through a single carrier.

The HR department also introduced a training module in recognition of the fact that peer training and informal chats with culture carriers aren't enough in the Information Age. Now the department oversees extensive in-person and online training sessions provided through what we call PHLY U. We also offer tuition reimbursement for outside accredited degree programs.

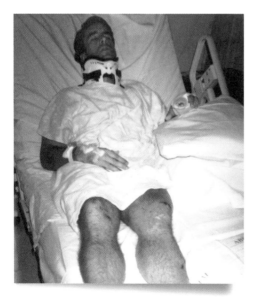

▶ **September 1, 2001 bike accident**
Jamie recovered in six months, and in 2003 completed the Ironman, Lake Placid.

A Sad and Scary September

All that I had worked for nearly flew apart on the morning of September 1, 2001, when Jamie was hit by a car during an early morning bicycle ride. Possibly blinded by the sunlight, neither Jamie nor the driver ever saw the other one coming. Jamie was catapulted into the air and did a couple of flips before landing on the

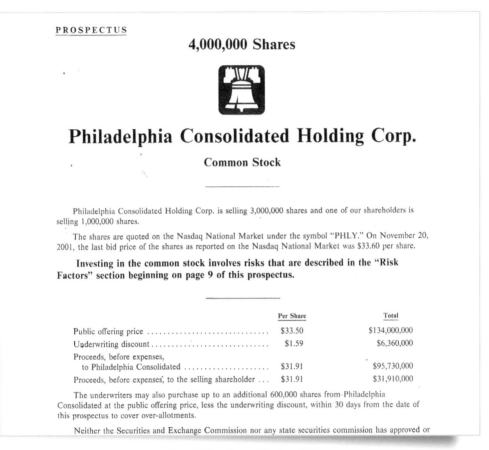

PROSPECTUS

4,000,000 Shares

Philadelphia Consolidated Holding Corp.

Common Stock

Philadelphia Consolidated Holding Corp. is selling 3,000,000 shares and one of our shareholders is selling 1,000,000 shares.

The shares are quoted on the Nasdaq National Market under the symbol "PHLY." On November 20, 2001, the last bid price of the shares as reported on the Nasdaq National Market was $33.60 per share.

Investing in the common stock involves risks that are described in the "Risk Factors" section beginning on page 9 of this prospectus.

	Per Share	Total
Public offering price	$33.50	$134,000,000
Underwriting discount	$1.59	$6,360,000
Proceeds, before expenses, to Philadelphia Consolidated	$31.91	$95,730,000
Proceeds, before expenses, to the selling shareholder	$31.91	$31,910,000

The underwriters may also purchase up to an additional 600,000 shares from Philadelphia Consolidated at the public offering price, less the underwriting discount, within 30 days from the date of this prospectus to cover over-allotments.

Neither the Securities and Exchange Commission nor any state securities commission has approved or

▸ Four Million Share Offering - 2001

car's windshield and then bouncing to the pavement. His bike was suspended overhead, tangled in power lines, and his neck, jaw, kneecaps, toes, and hand were broken.

He spent the next six months intermittently in and out of rehabilitation and was at home watching television the day the World Trade Towers fell. He lay suspended between his very real physical pain and a state of shock and disbelief at what he was seeing on television. His knowledge of the carnage and death of so many innocent people left him feeling helpless and devastated. The office of Sandler O'Neill, with whom we did business, was on the 100th floor of the World Trade Center. PHLY did not insure large property risks in metropolitan New York, which was of little comfort. Our small-business accounts (i.e., health clubs, social-service entities, daycare centers, etc.) sustained about $20 million of damage, mostly from soot clogging their air-conditioning systems. We promptly paid those losses and then stepped back to assess how this event would play out in the industry and for PHLY.

Two very significant events took place following the September 11th terrorist attacks.

First - The terrorist attacks had the immediate effect of reducing the industry's capital, thus Wall Street was open to new offerings. We seized this opportunity, because we were anticipating business growth. Our projections told us that new capital would eventually be needed. PHLY visited Wall Street again, this time to raise $130 million.

▶ Jamie as new CEO October 2002

On November 20, 2001, Merrill Lynch and the Bank of America prepared a four million-share public offering of PHLY stock. After a five-day road show, the offering was fully subscribed. One million shares were mine, with proceeds netting the company approximately $100 million and an additional $30 million to me.

Second - Ten months after the public offering, Jamie was promoted to CEO (October 2002). There were several factors that pushed that decision. In early 2002 I had a myocardial block which was induced by muscle spasms. On January 20th a stent was implanted in my left artery which put me on the sidelines for several weeks. This caused me to think about succession. Also, in the latter part of the year, I was asked by the president of Saint Joseph's University, Father Nicholas Rashford, S.J., to present a case study to MBA students. The topic: "When does the founder and CEO step aside."

I was 68 years old and was fairly sure that Jamie would be taking over as the next CEO. However, they did offer some interesting nuggets of wisdom: Step aside while you're young enough to still be engaged with what's going on in your company, your industry, and on Wall Street. Figure that you'll need to stick around for at least 48 months to ensure a smooth transition. Transfer the top job when you're sure the new CEO is ready, willing, and able.

I had no doubt that Jamie was up to the job but had not considered the importance of a transition period. So, in October 2002, I promoted him to the top job. He enthusiastically accepted the title of CEO at an elaborate dinner at the Ritz-Carlton Hotel in Philadelphia. All of our board members, national and regional vice presidents, investment bankers, and their spouses were on hand to hear me introduce Jamie. (Ruth had passed away on April 19, 2002, at age 95, and I deeply regretted that she couldn't be there to witness "the changing of the guard," something we had talked about on several occasions.)

Jamie accepted the position in a speech that mixed humor and humility with a heartwarming tribute to his father and an acknowledgement of what lies at the core of our success. Here is part of what he said that day:

I am humbled and honored to be chosen as the new CEO of such a dynamic, successful company. I am honored to be partners in business with all of you here tonight, and I am especially proud to work by the side of our chairman, who started with a simple dream and has built a national insurance powerhouse!

The leadership, discipline, and ingenuity he's shown over the last 42 years is truly remarkable, and what he has accomplished is nothing short of incredible ... To chart a course for where we're going, I find myself looking backwards ... trying to incorporate the lessons of the past, so that we avoid rough seas, keep our sails full, and continue on our journey safely. I'd be foolish not to consider how we've gotten to this point ... and I've distilled our historical success down to three simple characteristics on which I will continue to focus ... people, principles, and profitability.

October 2002

▸ **CEO Dinner - Bank of America Investment Bankers**
(left to right) Patricia and George Luecke, John and Franny Glomb, Jacque and Rob Giammarco, Tony and Kristin Ursano

No discourse before a room that includes your bankers would be complete without a nod to continued profitable growth, which Jamie attributed to "three simple things – execution, execution, execution." As he drew to a close, he spoke directly to me, thanking me for my "past leadership ... continuing counseling, and ... confidence ... I promise I won't screw it up!"

As I recalled the evolution in Jamie's career and how my confidence in him allowed him to forge his own path that eventually led him back to our family business, I remembered the confidence my own father instilled in me as I matured into a young man. As a father, I was enormously proud to see my son step into my shoes, especially since I knew that, in some ways, he was better qualified for the job than I.

Was I altogether happy about stepping aside? No, the decision was the toughest of my career and a bittersweet moment; I loved my job, I love PHLY, and just as important, I love the hundreds of kids I've brought into our company. But my own instincts and the considered advice of my board had convinced me that making way for Jamie was the right thing to do for the company.

The Perfect Storm

Following our successful Wall Street offering, we decided that our marketing strategy would remain unchanged. This would prove to be a stroke of genius, and was completely counter-intuitive in an industry which, because of its loss of capital caused by 9/11, was raising prices by 25 percent and higher. Our rates at the time were fair and adequate, and **gouging our costumers (just because we could) was not part of our culture!**

As 2002 dawned, there was a series of events that took place in the industry which created new and unexpected opportunities for PHLY. The high rates charged by competitors had the almost immediate dual-effect of chasing new customers to PHLY and helping us retain well over 90 percent of our existing accounts.

Industry Dislocation

During the next few years, we witnessed some of the most unprecedented industry dislocations of the past 100 years. Frontier and Legion Insurance Companies, two fierce competitors, were suspended from writing business by their state insurance departments. Their suspension was followed by the bankruptcy of Reliance and Kemper Insurance Companies, two of the oldest insurance companies in America. Immediately on the heels of these competitors going "down," came the four multibillion-dollar hurricanes of 2004, which severely impacted the capital adequacy of the industry.

In the space of three years, four major competitors went out of business and the hurricanes caused substantial capital drain, thus creating a "perfect storm" of tremendous opportunity for PHLY.

At the end of 2001, immediately after completing our public offering, our revenue was $336 million. Twenty-four months later, revenues had doubled to $620 million. Despite reduced competition, we kept our pricing stable, establishing a new level of broker and customer loyalty. Riding the crest of this growth, we added 150 new employees (underwriting and marketing), 58 new preferred agents, and opened six new offices.

In late 2004 CNA Financial Group agreed to purchase Continental Corp. for $1.1 billion, creating the nation's seventh largest insurance group. The acquisition was approved in May 2005 and thereafter the company immediately announced their intent to exit the nonprofit social service business – eliminating yet another PHLY competitor.

From 2005 to 2007 we continued to ride the wave of success. Revenue increased 50 percent to $1.53 billion with a combined ratio of 74.3 percent and earnings per share increased 100 percent to $4.64 from $2.29. With this remarkable run of growth, and bottom line profit, *Forbes* magazine in 2007 named PHLY as one of the 400 Best Big Companies in America.

As published in Forbes

*"The one thing
in life that's constant
is change!"*

James J. Maguire
Founder, Philadelphia Insurance Companies

Chapter 15
Transformational Years

OUR MISSION STATEMENT

- PHLY is a team of motivated high achievers committed to delivering innovative products and unsurpassed service to niche insurance markets.

- By maintaining a disciplined approach to business, we provide greater security for our policyholders and superior value for our shareholder.

- We believe that integrity and mutual respect are the foundation of long-term and fulfilling relationships with our employees, customers, and business partners.

"KAIZEN" 改善 – CONTINUOUS IMPROVEMENT

- Kaizen is a Japanese word meaning "continuous improvement," to which PHLY is committed in every aspect of its operations.

▶ **Our Mission Statement**

J amie's promotion to lead the company is probably one of my better management decisions. It didn't take Sean Sweeney by surprise, though he admitted to harboring hopes that he might someday be CEO. He soon realized that my choice was the right one; Jamie's style of leadership won him over.

My son and I have very different styles – each suited the company at different stages of its growth. I was tough, entrepreneurial, and demanding when that's what was required to grow and survive. Jamie is team oriented, collaborative, and low key. Technology and process are hugely important to him, but the company's technological advancements came about because management saw that technology promised control and openness at the same time.

Rather than give the management team orders, Jamie views them as equals. He looks to them to tell him what needs to be done. He often says that there is more to running a company than just bringing in business. The entire process is important. The company's longstanding procedure of reviewing enterprise risk management was substantially improved in 2003 when he hired Jim Tygh as our first chief actuarial officer. Over the course of the next seven years, Jim's role in bringing data analysis to the forefront has enabled PHLY management to act more decisively and get out ahead of the curve. Management committees initiated in the early 1990s, such as litigation review, product development, underwriting, and compliance issues, never vary. Monthly meetings are still the preferred venue.

The company intranet was initially started to share underwriting guidelines but has since been expanded to keep everyone up-to-date on important issues. Jamie also connects with all PHLY employees via Webcast at least twice a year.

▸ 2003 - PHLY fitness culture goes to the next level.
Tim Maguire, senior vice president; Cynthia Lasprogata, vice president; Debbie Sutton, senior vice president; and Jamie, CEO, compete at the 2003 Lake Placid Ironman and raise $75,000 for Children's Hospital.

Athletics and charitable giving have lost no currency over the years. If anything, the desire to compete and give back has only grown stronger. Employees of all ages and physical abilities run 5K races, marathons, and triathlons to raise money for worthy causes.

I do my part to keep our competitive culture strong by training every day with employees in the company health club, competing in the annual PHLY Triathlon and other local events, and celebrating the achievements of others. After Jamie, Tim, Debbie Sutton, and Cynthia Lasprogata (a vice president in our claims department), completed the 2003 Lake Placid Ironman race, raising $75,000 for the Children's Hospital in Philadelphia, I ordered four giant-sized cakes for a company party. It was the first time that four officers of the company had competed together in an Ironman, and I thought they deserved to hear the cheers of our admiring staff. None cheered louder than I did, especially when our CEO, who lay broken on the pavement just two years earlier, entered the room.

In February 2003, after reporting our year-end 2002 results to Wall Street, I received a call from Allison Jacobowitz, an analyst at Merrill Lynch. When I answered, she said, "No, Jim, I want to talk to the CEO." That was the moment I truly understood the torch had been passed.

The transformation in the intervening six years has been nothing short of spectacular. When listing the statistics below, it is with great pride that I commend the young men and women of PHLY for their leadership. They joined together – each office, each manager, each employee – to turn our aspirations into reality: They truly have taken the company to the next level.

Little wonder, then, that I relented when our management team asked me in December 2007 to at least hear out and consider opportunities that Merrill Lynch found very attractive. Who could question the judgment of a group that over the past six years had increased our bottom line by 1,000 percent?

▶ **Opening NASDAQ 2005**
(left to right) Jim Tygh, NASDAQ VP, John Shipley, Susie, Bill Benecke, Craig Keller, Jamie, Sean Sweeney, Debbie Sutton, Chris and Ellen Maguire, Joe Barnholt

Philadelphia Insurance Companies Financial Results - Rated A+

(In Thousands)

	2002	2003	2004	2005	2006	2007
▶ Company Assets	$ 1,358,000	$ 1,869,000	$ 2,500,000	$ 2,928,000	$ 3,439,000	$ 4,100,000
▶ Gross Written Premium	$ 663,739	$ 905,993	$ 1,171,317	$ 1,264,915	$ 1,493,248	$ 1,692,223
▶ Net Income	$ 33,753	$ 62,187	$ 83,683	$ 156,688	$ 288,849	$ 326,813
▶ Statutory Combined Ratio**	91.5%	90.3%	88.7%	78.1%	68.3%	74.3%
▶ Offices	36	37	38	38	39	47
▶ Niche Products	71	72	85	85	99	102
▶ Policyholders	55,800	73,900	92,000	108,300	150,100	287,850

As a public company, we had investment bankers calling us regularly. Were we interested in buying some other business that was up for sale? Did we want to raise new capital? Would we be willing to engage in exploratory conversations with a potential acquirer?

"Not interested," was my usual response. I never wanted our company name bandied about on the street as a willing acquisition target. A rumor like that might scare off business, and more importantly I didn't want to waste time in dead-end discussions.

I softened my stance somewhat after Jamie got to know and respect Dan Luckshire from Merrill Lynch. Like his fellow bankers, Dan regularly called on us to take the pulse of our company and update us on industry activities. In fall 2007 he told Jamie that a number of strong foreign companies were looking to enter the U.S. market. I dismissed that news, believing it to be a sales ploy to win permission to peddle our company abroad. But Luckshire persisted, pointing out to Jamie

▶ **Jamie, Jim, Tara, Susie - The culture of competition**
2006 Olympic distance triathlon benefiting Children's
Hospital of Philadelphia

and Chris at a December meeting that the shrinking U.S. dollar made it economically attractive for overseas companies to acquire U.S. insurers.

Intrigued by Luckshire's pitch, Jamie, Chris, and Craig wanted to know more about the foreign companies. It couldn't hurt, they argued, to look at four or five candidates. After all, we'd just be looking. "Okay," I said, "but don't waste my time on bottom feeders." I also made two things very clear up front: First, our selling price was three times our book value, and, second, there would be no deal unless the buyer agreed to keep our management team in place and in charge, doing business under the Philadelphia Insurance name.

In truth, I felt no need to make any move at all. The Maguire family owned 17 million shares of a company with zero debt and a long history of besting the competition. I felt like we were at the top of our game. It would, however, be interesting to learn how the market valued us, and I thought the exercise would show my sons that I had confidence in their management skills and respect for their opinions.

With 49 offices across the United States, a respected brand, a 10-year average combined claims and expense ratio of 85 percent, and revenues topping $1.7 billion annually, joining hands with the Philadelphia Insurance Companies would be a boon to any corporation looking for a toehold in the American market. Our compound annual growth rate over the preceding decade was 31.5 percent, and we projected our net income to continue growing at double-digit rates for at least another five years. The possibility of expanding outside the U.S. had been discussed with our board. But the timing wasn't right without either an international partner or an infusion of new capital, both of which a strong partner may bring to our company.

Integrity had always been the cornerstone of Tokio, and that was a key consideration for us.

The first option came to the fore after Merrill proposed three candidates, one of which was Tokio Marine. This was the same company that supported us with reinsurance on the four hurricanes in Florida in 2004. The professionalism and speed of service demonstrated by them at that time spoke volumes about the culture of their company, so when they were presented, it didn't take long to establish a high level of comfort. It was Japan's oldest insurance company, having been founded in 1879, with $172.5 billion in assets, 21,500 employees, and operations in 37 countries. More importantly, after completing our due diligence, we were hugely impressed with their underwriting record and reputation as insurance professionals. Their culture appeared to complement ours. Indeed, integrity had always been the cornerstone of Tokio, and that was a key consideration for us. As we later discovered, they felt much the same way about us and had been eyeing Philadelphia Insurance as a possible acquisition target for some time.

It was Japan's oldest insurance company, having been founded in 1879, with $172.5 billion in assets, 21,500 employees, and operations in 37 countries.

Tokio, as we quickly realized, is made up of first-class people who push themselves as hard as we do. Both companies are driven to succeed, which fosters respect and camaraderie, and both exhibit an intensity and motivation that spills onto the playing field. Tokio's CEO was an oarsman, skier, and rugby player, and he continues to be a competitive golfer.

As we learned more about Tokio, we had a strong sense that its management would welcome our culture. If anything, our cultural differences would be a plus for both companies. We envisioned opportunities to do business with Japanese-American brokers and to gain entrée into other countries

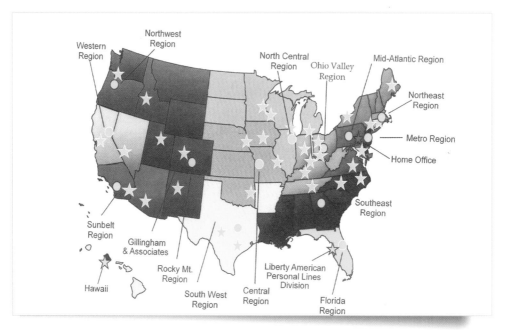

▸ **49 offices - 13 regions across the U.S.**

where we had no previous connection. For Tokio, establishing a substantial presence in the U.S. insurance market – the strongest in the world – made sound business sense.

On April 10, 2008, some weeks after Merrill Lynch's Japan office first contacted Tokio Marine, a team of executives came calling. They wanted to meet us in person and to learn more about our niche marketing, operations, and strategy. They liked what they saw, so we told them our price: $65 a share, or a total of $5 billion in cash.

The figure was important to me. Admittedly, our stock had recently traded down from $48.00 to below $33, but our track record and the fact that we were poised to continue

▶ **Firemark Plaque**
I presented our Firemark to Mr. Sumi as a symbol of our new relationship.

growing at 10 to 20 percent a year for the next five years, strengthened my resolve that the company was worth every bit of $65 a share. My asking price amounted to three times the company's book value of $21.64 a share as of March 31, 2008, and about double our stock price – multiples that no insurance company had ever gotten in a sale.

At a follow-up meeting in mid-May, we were invited to come to Tokyo to meet Tokio's senior management. Sure, we said. How about if we come in June? "Why not next weekend?" They countered. That's when we knew they were eager to do a deal.

Jamie, Chris, Craig, and Sean joined me on the long flight from Philadelphia that arrived in Tokyo on May 22.

At Tokio Marine's 23rd-floor headquarters, we were greeted with the formality typical of Japanese business meetings. Introduced first to the management team, we took part in an elaborate tea ceremony known as chanoyu, after which we were ushered into the offices of Shuzo Sumi, the company's president, where we exchanged pleasantries. Our next stop was the boardroom, which overlooked the Imperial Palace and was but a few blocks from the Ginza district, the center of Tokyo shopping and nightlife. It brought back memories of my military days.

Seating ourselves in the boardroom, we were careful to place me in the middle of the conference table, directly across from Shuzo Sumi, with Jamie and Sean seated on my right and Craig and Chris on my left. Before going to Tokyo we had hired a Japanese consultant to brief us on etiquette and business procedures, including seating rituals. I made a brief introduction, then turned the meeting over to Jamie, Sean, Chris, and Craig, each of whom took part in the presentation. After Sean described our Preferred Agent and Firemark programs, I rose and presented Sumi-san with a Philadelphia Insurance Companies Firemark Plaque, which we give to new agents as a symbol of our affiliation. "I hope this meeting is the prelude to a new relationship," I told him.

Afterwards, we were treated to an excellent, 13-course traditional Japanese dinner. Sumi-san graciously explained each course, toasted to our health, and thanked us for coming to Tokyo. The vintage sake was flowing freely, and the group enjoyed several bottles. As the evening wound down, Sean, clearly feeling the sake, raised his glass to toast our host and voiced his affection for his new acquaintances. "I love you guys!" he exclaimed. The six Tokio executives appeared to be relaxed and enjoying the camaraderie. All of the formality of the afternoon was gone. It felt like a night out with the guys.

Back at the Imperial Hotel, the five of us sat and talked for a half-hour, recapping the events of the day and unanimously agreeing that, from all appearances, these were people with integrity and a long-term view that fit our culture. We told Dan Luckshire that we wanted to hold off on any more meetings with a second suitor until we knew the outcome of the Tokio

▸ **The Tokyo visit 2008**

(clockwise seated - front center) Craig Keller; Ian Brimecome, financial advisor to Tokio Marine; Jim; Jamie; Chris, and Sean *(left to right, standing)* Toshiro Yagi, executive vice president; Daisaku Honda, executive vice president; Shuzo Sumi, president; Shin-Ichiro Okada, senior managing executive officer; Daniel Luckshire, Merrill Lynch; and Kunihiko Fujii, executive officer

▶ Imperial Hotel, May 2008

(left to right) Dan Luckshire of Merrill Lynch, Chris, Sean, Jim, Jamie, Craig

Marine negotiations. The second group, which we called "Party B," had been pushing to come to Philadelphia to ramp up our talks. But we all agreed that night if Tokio Marine met our number, we wanted to join forces.

You can imagine our surprise and consternation when, six days later, Tokio's senior managers appeared at our Bala Cynwyd headquarters with a $55-a-share offer that their representatives deemed "very attractive," indicating they were unlikely to go higher. We let two days go by before politely dismissing this unsatisfactory bid, and then sat back to see what would happen next.

Two weeks later, on June 16, the Fox-Pitt Kelton team, which was representing Tokio and led by Ian Brimecome, returned to our offices. At a previous meeting, we had collegially sung "Happy Birthday" to Tokio's managing director, the 58-year-old Shin-Ichiro Okada. And after the cake was cut, I had told Dan Luckshire to make it clear that we needn't meet again unless they were ready to pay our asking price. So with their return came a heightened expectation that they were ready to proceed. But as Ian presented the group's final offer, I froze. It was only $60 a share. Pushing back my chair, I stood up, excused myself, and left the room without saying a word.

Jamie, Sean, Craig, and Chris immediately followed me back to my office. Once inside, I said we would not accept the offer, and, though disappointed, everyone agreed. Offering $60 a share, or roughly $4.59 billion, after I had clearly and emphatically stipulated $65 was a clear sign to me that the deal was likely dead.

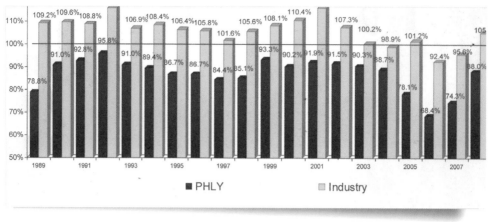

Industry vs PHLY Combined Loss and Expense Ratio

▸ PHLY outperformed the industry by an average of 15% for 20 consecutive years

Dan privately told Brimecome that we didn't have a deal. I had urged Dan to be diplomatic because I wanted the Japanese to understand that we had great respect for them and harbored no bad feelings. But the only acceptable number remained $65.

In an odd way, I was actually relieved that the meetings and negotiations appeared to be over. My life's work was up for bid, and I felt strongly that we had the best business model in the industry. We could look forward to more years of double-digit growth, continuing our 48-year run of success. We could now forget about selling or merging the company and get back to work.

Two weeks later, Brimecome and the Tokio management team were back again, their sixth visit. Brimecome said Tokio couldn't get to $65, but asked if we would consider coming down slightly. Okay, I replied, but $63.50 was as low as we would go. Much to my dismay, they countered yet again, this time making what they termed their "final offer" of $61.50. This equated to a total cash offer of $4.74 billion and represented an 85 percent premium over the then-current stock price and 2.81 times our book value.

Again, we paraded out of the conference room and over to my office, this time to huddle and debate the latest proposal. In no time, the discussion grew heated. My position was "no deal!" Jamie argued that the offer was a good one from a highly reputable, financially strong company with a global presence and resources to help us reach our full potential. "They were smart to do this deal, and we would be dumb to reject it," Jamie said. Chris and Craig seconded Jamie's opinion. It was Sean who got my undivided attention, though: "Are you being a pig?" he asked bluntly.

Money was never the issue for me, and, frankly, it did not matter to me whether the deal went through or not. But Sean's question made me realize that the company wasn't mine alone

> **The closing dinner, December 1, 2008**
> Chris, Sean, Jim, Shuzu Sumi, Jamie, Craig

anymore. Jamie, Chris, Sean, and Craig were running it, and they wanted to do the Tokio deal. And what drove them was an attitude I had spent much time instilling in them – and for one big reason: It was my father's gift to me. I had handed down his legacy of self-confidence, of having faith in your ability to dedicate your life to something big, and to persist and overcome any adversity on the way to your own personal pinnacle.

The deal was struck with a handshake on the afternoon of June 30, 2008, partnering PHLY with a global company and moving Tokio Marine a huge step forward in its quest to become a U.S. insurance powerhouse. After three weeks of intense due diligence, both companies executed the acquisition agreement. On July 23, 2008, Tokio marine announced that it would pay $4.74 billion in cash for Phly or $61.50 per share, which was a 73% premium to the company's closing price of $35.55 the previous day.

Timing is everything it's been said, and so it was with the acquisition of our company. Less than two months after announcing our deal, the financial markets on Wall Street started to come unraveled with the bankruptcy of Lehman Brothers, the sale of Merrill Lynch to Banc of America followed by the troubled Asset Relief Program (TARP) announced in October, a program of the United States Government to purchase assets and equity from financial institutions to strengthen its financial sector. It was the largest component of the U.S. government's measure in 2008 to address the subprime mortgage crisis.

I wish I could say that our decision to sell the company when we did had something to do with our knowledge of the financial markets. The truth is we didn't! To the credit of Tokio Marine, when the markets crashed, they never once suggested or inferred that they wanted to

The Philadelphia Inquirer

Bala Cynwyd insurer is sold

Philadelphia Consolidated Holding, around since the 50's, is to be bought by Tokio Marine Holdings for $4.7 billion cash

By Harold Brubaker
Inquirer Staff Writer

James J. Maguire had his first success in insurance by using sign language to sell life insurance to deaf people in the late 1950s.

Now, he is selling what he built into a publicly traded insurance company in Bala Cynwyd to a Japanese insurance giant for $4.7 billion in cash, one of the largest deals ever by a Japanese buyer in the United States, according to Standard & Poor's.

Tokio Marine Holdings Inc. said yesterday that it would pay $61.50 per share for Philadelphia Consolidated Holding Corp. The price is 73 percent more than the Company's closing price Tuesday of $35.55.

Shares in the Company, which specializes in niche products, such as insurance for adoption agencies, closed yesterday at $58.43, up 22.88 or 64 percent. The stock has risen an average of 17 percent annually for the last decade, compared with 2.7 percent for the Standard & Poor's 500-stock index.

"It's been a great experience to take the business from scratch, starting with my wife as my secretary," Maguire, 74, said in an interview yesterday. "I'm only mad about one thing. I wish I was 20 years younger."

Maguire said he has agreed to remain chairman for three years and will invest in Tokio Marine.

The sale of Philadelphia Consolidated is the second large deal this month involving a Philadelphia-area firm with large stock holdings still in the hands of a founding family. The other involved Rohm & Haas Co., which agreed to a $15 billion buyout by Dow Chemical Co. two weeks ago.

One thing that has not changed at Philadelphia Consolidated is family involvement. Four of Maguire's eight children work there, as well as a cousin and a son-in-law. The firm employs 600 in Bala Cynwyd and 1,400 at 47 offices nationwide.

Jamie Maguire, a son who is chief executive and has an employment agreement with Tokio Marine, said he expected business as usual — and faster growth. "Since Tokio Marine has such a small U.S. operation, it allows us to continue to run the Company and be their platform for the U.S," the younger Maguire said.

Left to right: Mr. James Maguire, Founder
Mr. Jamie Maguire, President and CEO

Philadelphia Consolidated started looking for "potential partners" in February for help growing, particularly outside the United States, Jamie Maguire, 48, said. "We've always had our sights across the border," he said.

Other top executives have also agreed to stay on after the deal's close, expected in the fourth quarter. Both boards of directors have approved the deal, whose total value is $4.7 billion. It awaits approval by Philadelphia Consolidated shareholders.

The Maguire family, with 18 percent of Philadelphia Consolidated's shares, worth nearly $800 million at the sale price, has already said it would vote in favor of the deal, Tokio Marine said.

This has been a slow-growth period for insurance companies, which have been forced to consider merging in order to maintain premium growth and market share, experts said. Many deals are expected to cross international borders.

The weak dollar helps, but "it's . . . also a question of where someone like Tokio Marine can get growth," said Michael Costonis, a Philadelphia-based senior executive in Accenture's global insurance practice.

The United States is the largest market for property and casualty insurance in the world, according to Tokio Marine, which calls itself the largest property and casualty insurer in Japan.

John Swanick, senior managing director at Smart Business Advisory & Consulting L.L.C. in Devon, said the deal will be good for both companies by giving Tokio Marine a significant presence in the United States while Philadelphia Consolidated gets access to international markets.

Despite a new international bent, Jamie Maguire said Philadelphia Consolidated would continue sponsoring the Philadelphia Triathlon and other athletic events in the region.

> The deal gives Tokio Marine a presence in the U.S.; Philadelphia Consolidated gets access to global markets.

▸ $4.7 billion

▶ **December 2008**
Mr. Sumi, president, and Mr. Ishihara, chairman of Tokio Marine Insurance, come to Philadelphia
and present a painting of Mt. Fuji

rethink or renegotiate our deal. Their decision to acquire PHLY was unwavering, which speaks volumes about the integrity of our new partners.

Their efforts have paid off handsomely, as evidenced by another banner year for PHLY in 2008. On December 31, 2008, more than six months after the merger and with competition in the marketplace increasing, we posted 12 percent growth in gross written premiums, which reached almost $1.9 billion. Our statutory combined ratio, excluding merger costs, was 83.4 percent, while net income, including $62.5 million of after-tax merger-related expenses, totaled $223.7 million.

Spirits were running high on the night of December 1 when my family and staff members celebrated our union with the Tokio board and other company representatives at the Four Seasons in Philadelphia. Jamie was especially excited by the opportunity the merger provided to move our company onto the international stage.

What drove them was an attitude I had spent much time instilling in them.

For me and my family, netting almost one billion dollars was clearly a big payday. The money however took a back seat to the knowledge that the Philadelphia Insurance name would live on, with some complement of Maguires running the business. It was in all ways a dream come true. We have been blessed and I am a fortunate man.

"When you do your best with what you have,

it's not the getting – but the trying that brings joy"

James J. Maguire
Founder, Philadelphia Insurance Companies

Epilogue
Family Album

▶ Franny, Megan, Tim, Frannie, Chris, Jamie, Colleen, Tara, Jim, Susie

J amie's achievements have been duly recognized in this book, as have Chris and Tim's.

But I am equally proud of all my children. Each has excelled in his or her own way while taking different paths.

Susie, who directed public relations at the company, is one of the family's best runners and an all-around great athlete.

Megan and Colleen are the only two of my children who escaped the clutches of the family insurance business. They are well-adjusted and successful in their own vocations. Meg is the mother of five children and the wife of Mark, himself a successful entrepreneur. She is an

▶ Susie Maguire

avid biker and runner and is a newly fledged elementary school teacher. She earned her master's degree in education from Saint Joseph's University in 2008.

Colleen ran her own beauty-salon business before selling it to devote herself full-time to her two children. She's participated in the annual Philadelphia Insurance triathlon.

Little Franny, who manages the Maguire Educational Foundation, graduated from the University of Pennsylvania in 1994. Franny came to the company in 1996 and trained as an underwriter in Jamie's division. She put her knowledge to work by establishing a professional liability underwriting unit in our San Francisco office.

Franny's westward journey was precipitated by her 1998 marriage to John Glomb, her college sweetheart, who was chosen to manage AIG's San Francisco office. Though John's career at AIG could never be attributed to nepotism, it was Jamie who hired John in 1994 to work in AIG's professional liability division. John subsequently earned an MBA from the Wharton School and went to work for Tony Ursano at the Bank of America. The Franny/John/Jamie circle was closed in 2007, when John left Bank of America to become Philadelphia Insurance's vice president of underwriting, quickly rising to senior vice president.

For years, I viewed my art form to be the Philadelphia Insurance Companies ...

Tara, the All-American Penn State field hockey player, temporarily left school to play on the 1996 U.S. Olympic team in Atlanta. She subsequently completed her degree and went on to earn an MBA from Saint Joe's. Tara followed her siblings' lead, taking a position for a time in our Laguna Beach office managed by her brother Tim before returning to school to get a master's degree in psychology, the field in which she now works.

To date, Frannie and I have been blessed with 21 grandchildren. When we are not enjoying the frequent company of our children and grandchildren, we pursue our own interests. Frannie maintains an art studio in our home, where she paints and sculpts on a regular basis. Her most recent achievement was sculpting the bust of Anthony Cardinal Bevilacqua, retired Archbishop of Philadelphia. I keep abreast of the business in my position as chairman emeritus, and I always find time to work out at the office gym. I enjoy hanging out with my younger colleagues, because it pushes me to work harder.

Frannie and I still adhere to the Jesuit philosophy of being dedicated to others, which guides our charitable activities in education, the arts, and medicine. We still love to travel. We enjoy golfing and bike tours. We've pedaled from coast to coast in the U.S. and across Europe, from Nova Scotia to New Zealand and points in between.

I have very few regrets as I move to the next chapter of my life. My Dad never had a chance to see the fruits of his labor and the profound impact he made on my life. I also regret that my Mom, who was part of my early business career, wasn't here to see the company she loved transition into its new partnership with Tokio Marine. I'm sure she would have approved!

▸ **Franny Glomb**
2007 New York Marathon

▸ **Megan Maguire Nicoletti**
1998 Philadelphia Marathon

As Frannie and I contemplate the future, I look forward to new challenges. For years, I viewed my art form to be the Philadelphia Insurance Companies; however, I always knew that it was Frannie and my children who inspired me to believe and achieve. They, more than any thing or any other person, have made me proud to be a husband, father, and mentor.

I love my company and the men and women with whom I've been privileged to work. They will forever be my extended family.

In my effort to tell the story of the Philadelphia Insurance Companies and its unprecedented success, I know there are events, achievements and employees that are not mentioned. There were raw recruits who grew up to be leaders, and seasoned professionals who made strong contributions. Each carried part of the load and made the dream come true. It's because of them and with them that we did it!

A Culture of Fitness - Business and Family

▸ Chris Maguire
2007 PHLY Triathlon

▸ Tim Maguire
2007 PHLY Triathlon

▸ 1998 - Tara wins the Escape from
Alcatraz Triathlon

▸ John Glomb
2008 Pacific Half-Ironman

Field Leadership

▸ Robert Pottle, Tim Maguire, Bob O'Leary
National Managers

Management Team 2003

▶ Jamie, Craig, Sean, Chris

The Board of Directors 2008

▶ *(left to right)* Michael Morris, Don Pizer, Paul Hertel, Betsy Gimmel, Sean Sweeney, James Maguire, Jamie Maguire, Ron Rock, Shaun O'Malley, Mike Cascio, Amenta H. Brough

Thanks to our Board for their support and counsel.

Prior Board Members: Helping to Shape PHLY

▸ Rohit Desai
10/86 - 9/93

▸ William J. Henrich, Jr.
7/96 - 4/05

▸ Roger Larson
7/85 - 4/01

▸ Margaret M. Mattix
2/03 - 10/06

▸ Maureen H. McCullough
10/02 - 4/05

▸ Thomas J. McHugh
2/86 - 4/03

▸ Tom Nerney
7/85 - 5/96

▸ Dirk A. Stuurop
10/99 - 9/02; 2/04 - 4/06

▸ J. Eustace Wolfington
2/86 - 4/05

▸ James J. Zech
7/01 - 4/03

2010 Philadelphia Triathlon

▶ Masa and Kate Nomoto, Mark Yoda, Jamie Maguire,
Eugene Nomura, Daisuke Yagaki, Masashi "Kobe" Kobayashi

In January 2010 I relinquished my position as chairman to Jamie, and agreed to remain on the PHLY board as an advisor. The company is in the able hands of our partners at Tokio Marine and the PHLY management team. The opportunities for continued growth abound as the cultures of the two companies come together. Already, the fitness culture at PHLY has captured our partners, as evidenced by their participation in the annual Philadelphia Triathlon and other similar events.

December 2008

$4,709,432,711

PHILADELPHIA CONSOLIDATED HOLDING CORP.

has been acquired by

TOKIO MARINE HOLDINGS, INC.

The undersigned acted as exclusive financial advisor
to Philadelphia Consolidated Holding Corp.

Merrill Lynch